LEVERAGING
THE HORIZON

SECRETS OF A SERIAL ENTREPRENEUR

LEVERAGING
THE HORIZON

SECRETS OF A SERIAL ENTREPRENEUR

BY EDWIN R. ADDISON
FOREWORD BY GUY KAWASAKI

Writers Advantage
New York Lincoln Shanghai

Leveraging the Horizon
Secrets of a Serial Entrepreneur

Writers Advantage
an imprint of iUniverse, Inc.

For information address:
iUniverse
2021 Pine Lake Road, Suite 100
Lincoln, NE 68512
www.iuniverse.com

ISBN: 0-595-26751-3 (Pbk)
ISBN: 0-595-65623-4 (Cloth)

Printed in the United States of America

To my beloved wife Kathy,
for her love and support as I went through this process.

Contents

A vision for a venture is not as simple as an idea. Ideas are a dime a dozen and in and of themselves are not of high value. A vision is more than an idea. A vision defines how a business concept and its implementation will be positioned in the market and how it will impact the world. Great businesses have great visions. This chapter looks at the aspects of generating, evolving, and crystallizing an effective vision for a technology venture.

One of the key themes throughout the book is that powerful teams are essential to the success of a venture. Both initial and extended teams are vitally important in the process of launching a vision. This chapter explores the issues involved in selecting the founding team, advisors, and early hires. It will also discuss how to motivate and integrate the team so the venture is driven forward powerfully and effectively.

"Leveraging the horizon" refers to establishing a point on the horizon as the ideal vision of a venture, then using that point as a beacon to guide you and your company. To achieve a breakthrough innovation, your hori-

viii Leveraging the Horizon

zon must be based on marketplace knowledge and be positioned somewhere between a bleeding-edge venture and me-too technology. And as
the horizon is always in the distance, your venture must undergo constant
innovation.

Chapter 4: Writing in the Sand 67
A business plan is an ongoing process, not an end product. Chapter 4
addresses the importance of the business plan and how its development
truly is a never-ending task, not an end product, and one that forces you
to continually keep an eye on the horizon.

Chapter 5: Sharpening the Ax 86
Chapter 5 focuses on the incubation of the venture and all the things that
need to be done before launching a major visible market penetration
effort. These include the preparation involved before implementing a
strategy, such as developing early alliances and beta sites and completing
prototypes.

Chapter 6: Designing the Culture 111
Designing your culture can be an important part of the implementation
and management of your business and the achievement of your venture's
objectives. This chapter discusses designing a culture that is consistent
with your horizon.

Chapter 7: Penetrating the Market 133
Penetrating the market is perhaps the most vital step in the survival of
your early stage technology venture. This chapter emphasizes that choosing and penetrating your beachhead market is intimately tied to a marketplace that benefits from your present offering and your ultimate horizon.
It addresses your competitive landscape and how to take the market lead.

Chapter 8: Funding the Venture 157

Seeking funding to build a venture is one of the most talked-about and misunderstood areas of interest among entrepreneurs. Many dream of landing a fistful of money but don't realize that raising money is extremely time-consuming and that more often than not the money goes to those who are already running a successful business. Chapter 8 provides insight into the world of financing your venture.

The preceding chapters have focused on how to start and build a new venture. Chapter 9 is about how to grow a company once it is established. It also addresses how to face competition and possible market erosion due to changes in the market or technology.

The minds of entrepreneurs, venture capitalists, employee-option holders, and investors are often driven by two words: exit strategy. This chapter is about how to recognize when it is time to deploy an exit strategy and what considerations should be made in executing the exit.

Acknowledgements

This book would not have been possible without the direct and indirect assistance of many others. Mostly, I would like to thank my wife, Kathy, and my children, Shelby, Lindsay, Evan, and Claire, for their patience as I wrote this book. I would like to make an additional note of thanks to Shelby, who did extensive proofreading on my original rough draft. I especially thank my editor and marketing assistant, Carol Dietch-Long, who did extensive copy editing and counsel regarding publishing and marketing. Thanks also to Guy Kawasaki of Garage Technology Ventures for his advice and his introduction. I also thank many business people who have reviewed the manuscript in advance of publication, including venture capitalist Stefan Strein, intellectual property counsel Lawrence Husick, and others who reviewed the writing, including Don Wilson, Gary Marple, Dan O'Neill, and Paul Nelson.

Then there are also those who have been vital to the success of the ventures that led up to this book, without whose success this book would not be possible. A partial list of them includes Paul Nelson, John McGrath, Don Wilson, Bob Kaminski, Ken Clark, Arden Blair, Terri Hobbs, Jim Blair, Don Tyson, Lawrence Husick, Bill Greenberg, Marvin Weinberger, Mark Gaertner, Ted Bagheri, Walter Hilton, Michael Gallagher, Wayne Lee, Sam Welshlager, David Chalk, Dave Judson, Dan O'Neill, and dozens of others who could not be listed here, but also deserve credit. There are many people to acknowledge in the writing of this book, not all of whom it is possible to mention here. I apologize to those who may have helped in some way that I did not mention by name here.

Foreword

I'm often asked the dos and don'ts of being an entrepreneur. How do I get started? What do I say to venture capitalists? What are the best market conditions for an entrepreneur? The good news is that, if you're an entrepreneur, it's always a good time to start a company. Conversely, if you're not an entrepreneur it's never a good time to start a company. Since you're reading this, we'll assume you're in the former category and tell you the other good news. You're holding a book that will offer you great insight to the awesome power of creating an enterprise and seeing it flourish.

Leveraging the Horizon takes a profound concept and shows how to apply it in the context of launching a venture. But don't be fooled. This is not a collection of simplistic "duhisms." Addison offers hard-core advice on everything from the getting started to crafting an exit.

Addison's concept of "leveraging the horizon" refers to establishing a point on the horizon as the ideal vision of your venture, then using that point as a beacon to guide you and your company. To achieve a breakthrough innovation, the point you establish, your horizon, must be based on marketplace knowledge and be positioned somewhere between a bleeding-edge venture and me-too technology. *Leveraging the Horizon* shows you how to use that vision and catapult it to build great teams, excite the marketplace, and squash the competition.

Entrepreneurs who succeed maintain focus on their horizon and jump the curve to achieve a breakthrough. Jump the curve is what Amazon.com did to bookselling. It's what refrigerator companies did to the ice industry when they built personal coolers, the industry's equivalent to PCs. It's what Federal Express did to the shipping industry. And the jump often is made by the people you would least expect.

The owners of the high-end photo labs, for example, didn't create one-hour developing. It's up to you. *Leveraging the Horizon* prepares you for the challenge and helps you to think differently to dominate the marketplace.

The key to success is to focus on stuff that's real: technology, people, and business models. *Leveraging the Horizon* shows you how to focus on the real and the ideal to achieve the best results.

Guy Kawasaki
Chairman and CEO
Garage Technology Ventures

Introduction

Great businesses begin with great visions. But can anyone with a great vision build a successful venture? The answer is yes—with the proper preparation, cultivation, and execution. There are many factors within your control to ensure your vision inspires a successful venture. What is unique about this book is that it offers you great insight into these factors that are in your control to give you awesome power. You will learn success factors that most entrepreneurs gain only by doing or through the "school of hard knocks." While no book can completely substitute for insight gained through experience, this is no ordinary business book. It differs from other books on entrepreneurship in its provision of hard-core advice combined with the powerful concept of leveraging your vision completely, rather than simply providing an encyclopedic accounting of the usual business topics that an entrepreneur might find useful.

You are about to embark on a journey in virtual experience. Along this journey, you will gain some valuable knowledge about the psychology, action steps, and frame of mind necessary to create high-potential ventures. However, you need not worry—you are not on the brink of reading yet another one of those uninventive how-to guides about writing a business plan or raising money. Instead, you will be exposed to a book that explains a philosophy—"leveraging the horizon"—and why this philosophy is an integral part to the success of any venture. While reading this book, you will take a look at several important factors necessary for the survival of a company in the business world. Some of these factors include the motivational issues involved in building a team, the highs and lows experienced by all entrepreneurs, and the driving factors required for a successful venture.

Since you are about to invest the time and energy to read this book, you deserve to be informed of my background experience as an entrepreneur. The basis for this book rests upon my experiences through two original ventures, three mergers and acquisitions, and over a dozen start-up companies to which I served as an advisor.

My career began with a traditional Fortune 500 job. I was an engineer at Westinghouse—a forever-frustrated engineer at that. The source of my frustration stemmed from several factors, but mostly from the strict organization that hindered me from realizing my potential. Bureaucratic hurdles, pecking orders, and other people waiting to benefit from my labor were just a few of the drawbacks involved in working at Westinghouse. After several years of work, I opted to take a sabbatical year and attend Massachusetts Institute of Technology as an industry fellow, where I studied artificial intelligence. Looking back on my year at MIT, I now realize that the most significant part of this experience was not so much the education, but more than that, my exposure to the contagious "entrepreneurial fever" that seems to pervade the air in Cambridge, Massachusetts. This exposure served to reinforce my internal desire to become an entrepreneur rather than to work for someone else's company.

After dealing with some unfinished business at Westinghouse, I spent a couple of years in management consulting at Booz, Allen & Hamilton. Here, everyone was responsible for bringing in his or her own business. This type of work environment provided me with the opportunity to learn about entrepreneurship within an organization. In addition to learning some of the talents of entrepreneurship at Booz, I was also exposed to ruthlessness at its very best—an experience that, while not entirely pleasant, had an imprinting effect on me, transforming me into a much more aggressive person business-wise and benefiting me in many other indirect ways.

During the time that I spent at Booz, I also taught part time at Johns Hopkins University as an adjunct professor of computer science. After awhile, I began to offer the courses I was teaching at Johns Hopkins University as commercially available industry short courses. At first I taught these courses through the university, but eventually I taught them independently. Through this experience, I improved my marketing skills and made some decent money on the side. In addition, the experience served as a positive reinforcement that helped to build my self-image as an entrepreneur, providing me with enough confidence that I believed nothing could stop me from venturing out to become an entrepreneur on my own.

Following my years at Booz, I founded ConQuest Software, a search engine company based on artificial intelligence technology. You will read a great deal about ConQuest throughout the book, but in a nutshell, the venture used an exotic data structure called a semantic network to improve search accuracy. ConQuest was a true example of "leveraging the horizon." In 1995, the company merged with Excalibur Technologies, now Convera (CNVR), and to this day it remains their flagship product. ConQuest was a venture that I entered blindly, yet succeeded at, as a result of my perseverance and ability to leverage the power of the raw technology available to my company.

After ConQuest, I went on to earn the title of serial entrepreneur by starting an Internet business information service called Powerize.com. This venture developed Internet portal software and then bought IBM infoMarket™ and Lotus Newsstand™[*] from the IBM Internet division in Falls Church, VA. Powerize.com merged with Hoovers, Inc. in Austin, Texas just prior to the infamous bursting of the Internet bubble. Although this venture was successful, its level of success did not match that of ConQuest. I think this inconsistency was due partially to the differing market conditions, but mostly to the fact that ConQuest had reached for

---

[*] infoMarket and Lotus Newsstand are trademarks of IBM Corporation.

a loftier horizon and had possessed the outstanding engineering required to reach this horizon. Despite its paling in comparison to ConQuest, Powerize.com was a great business platform for learning. We managed deals with AOL, Netscape, Inktomi, About.com, NBC, all of the major financial and news publishers, and numerous distributors. In addition, we raised angel money, institutional money, and filed to go public (but we chose to merge with Hoovers instead).

Subsequent to ConQuest and Powerize.com, I became an advisor to many start-up companies, aiding them in product positioning, structuring, fundraising, recruiting, and technology. I continue to advise several of these companies today.

Looking back on my work experiences, I believe that I learned about entrepreneurship from the school of hard knocks. Call it OJT (on-the-job training) if you will. At the time, I believed that this unnecessary torture was part of the process that every entrepreneur must go through. However, now that I have completed several ventures and succeeded through a process of trial and error, I realize that much of what I learned through experience could have been passed on to me by someone who had been there and done that before. With this notion in mind, I decided to write a book for the entrepreneurs in this world who might benefit from the words and experience of another. And thus, you have *Leveraging the Horizon*.

Throughout this book, examples are drawn from my personal venture experience as well as that of many other ventures, including well-known and not-so-well-known ones. Often, anecdotes involving specific persons are provided. In these instances, the persons depicted are often fictional, but represent events that actually occurred to one or more other persons. This method was used to avoid any accidental character references that are not intended. The sole purpose of such anecdotes is to help future entrepreneurs gain valuable experience by reading this book. Enjoy the journey!

Chapter 1

Inspiring the Vision

"Whatever the mind can conceive, the mind can achieve!"
—Napoleon Hill

"Leveraging the horizon"—you may ask, what exactly does it mean? First of all, every venture has a "horizon," an ultimate goal on which to place the focus of the venture. Experience has proven that there are two extreme types of ventures. The first extreme is a business with an exotic new horizon, one that is completely oblivious to today's world—rocket science, so to speak. This venture may go so far out on the bleeding edge that it hemorrhages to death. The other extreme type of venture is the "me-too" venture: "if Joe Blow can do it, so can I." This venture copies today's world and is not imaginative enough to seek a new horizon. Ultimately, it will become lost in the crowd. The ideal venture must fall between the two extremes described above. It must seek a horizon that is new and inventive, but one that is not so lofty as to be unattainable.

Now that we've discussed the horizon of a venture, it is now possible to understand the concept of "leveraging the horizon." This concept simply refers to the idea of working toward the horizon of your venture, while at the same time remaining on "terra firma" in today's marketplace. In other words, to reach the horizon, practical steps must be taken in the direction of the goal without sacrificing the stability of your venture.

In addition to explaining the philosophy of leveraging the horizon in this book, I have included a few supplementary ideas as well. As a result of my entrepreneurial experiences, I have concluded that there are several fundamental themes necessary for the success of any high potential venture. These themes, woven throughout the book, are:

- **Innovation:** Innovation can be planned by reaching for the ultimate goal ("the horizon") and leveraging that reach to find grounding in current reality. Innovation is critical to the launching of a worthy and successful venture.
- **Powerful Teams:** The key to success does not lie in being blessed with luck or the skill to utilize raw technology, but in the building of powerful teams. This skill requires equity motivation, properly balanced management style, unquestionable authority, and a clear vision.
- **Tenacious Execution:** Growing ventures to create real value requires steadfast, tenacious execution, resulting from an extreme level of perseverance that few people naturally possess.

However, the main focus of *Leveraging the Horizon* remains on the discussion of new high tech ventures and strategies for the practical execution of these ventures. The information and advice contained within this book is by no means limited to the next Microsoft-like venture—it pertains to the more typical high-tech ventures as well. Today, there are more high potential seeking start-up companies emerging than at any other time in history. Indeed, entrepreneurship is one of the foremost callings in the professional world these days. Most new technological ventures are founded by first-time entrepreneurs. Unfortunately, many of these ventures are founded on half-baked or "me-too" ideas, with substandard teams and poor execution that ultimately lead to less-than-optimal performance. It need not be that way! Buckle your seatbelt! The journey is about to begin…

Finding Inspiration

The key to success is in generating, evolving, and crystallizing an effective vision, combined with innovation and proper business positioning. A vision, however, is more than an idea. It is a strategic blueprint built within your imagination that outlines how you will break tradition and delve into new territory, either through technology, business concept innovation, or both. It paints a picture of how a business concept works, including the underlying technology of the venture, how the venture will be positioned in the market, and the impact it will have on the world. Your vision, more than anything else, will act as a magnet that attracts people to your venture, whether as employees, investors, or customers.

From where do great ideas come? Ideas are typically generated after gaining in-depth knowledge and thorough experience and developing a genuine interest in your chosen profession. However, you can plan for inspiration by creating an environment from which inspiration is derived.

> A vision is more than an idea. It is a strategic blueprint within your imagination that outlines how you plan to break tradition and delve into new territory, either through technology, business concept innovation, or both.

A background of progressively higher technical education, experience in a field, and exposure to customers is a rich ecosystem from which to draw ideas. If a brilliant idea is eluding you, you might try sharpening your technical education. Then work for someone so you can benchmark the current state of the industry and the specific needs of its audience. By being present in your field and observing your customers' needs, you will learn to recognize market trends. This process may seem to take a long time. It does—depending on from where you start. But the more deeply involved you become, the more readily good ideas will flourish.

Most high-tech entrepreneurs have majored in engineering, science, or a computer field. While the press is giddy with stories about college dropouts who go on to become billionaires, e.g. Bill Gates, the vast majority of entrepreneurs in the high-tech field are highly educated. The majority may not become billionaires, but the entrepreneurs who attain success undoubtedly become quite well off.

Entrepreneurs tend to share other traits beyond advanced education and technical experience. Many share common personality traits that help to inspire their vision and turn others into believers as well.

The Making of an Entrepreneur

Entrepreneurs seem to share a distinct set of character traits. Among these traits are confidence, charisma, tenacity, and zeal. These characteristics will influence everything from selling products to convincing someone to join the team, as well as acquiring a corporate partner, government contract, press appointment, or service provider. How many of these traits describe you? Or, more importantly, how many could you acquire if you were fully engaged in a compelling entrepreneurial activity?

The box below contains some characteristics of a typical entrepreneur. Although it can be argued that all entrepreneurs are different—and you don't have to possess these characteristics to succeed—you may want to use this list for self-assessment to capitalize on your strengths and work on your weaknesses.

COMMON PERSONALITY TRAITS OF ENTREPRENEURS
▪ Unrelenting confidence
▪ Belief in future success
▪ Excellent communicator and motivator
▪ Desire to change the world
▪ Passion for his or her chosen field
▪ Best salesman in the house
▪ A risk taker—not afraid to fail
▪ Driven to achieve goals
▪ Able to operate well in an uncertain environment
▪ Strong visionary, leader, and coach

Notice that eccentricity is missing from the list of traits. Many people mistakenly believe that eccentricity is a prerequisite to be an entrepreneur. This is not true. In fact, many highly celebrated entrepreneurs are not nearly as eccentric as the general public believes. Behavior that is highly organized and direct is mislabeled as eccentricity. People love anecdotes, however, and therefore the eccentric entrepreneur is indeed captivating. In *The New New Thing*, Michael Lewis describes the eccentricity of Jim Clark, the thrice billionaire ex-Stanford professor who founded Silicon Graphics, Netscape, and WebMD/Healtheon, and who will undoubtedly take the entrepreneurial route several more times.

There is no blueprint or stereotype that fits all entrepreneurs. We can, however, learn from the many who have achieved success. Many knowledgeable authors have written on the subject, such as Guy Kawasaki in *Rules for Revolutionaries*, James Cook in *The Start-up Entrepreneur*, and Carter Henderson in *Winners*.

One of the most important traits of all is passion. Passion for what you do and a drive to change the world are absolutely necessary if you are going to launch a venture. If you are in it just for the money or the power, you will run out of fuel and become demoralized when times get tough. It's the passion that keeps you going when everything else is stacked against you. It's the passion that sells your product. And it's contagious.

I realized this while at Powerize.com, an Internet business information service I founded in an attempt to do an early initial public offering (IPO) when the "dot-com" market had an insane capital market driving it. During the IPO process, which required many late night hours in lawyers' offices, I realized that I was chasing this IPO for the glory. The company had taken so many twists and turns in response to the changing market that I was no longer passionate about its product. I was selling an IPO, not a product. It made the challenging task of launching a venture much more difficult.

While you are assessing yourself, decide just how passionate you are about the business, venture, or product you plan to create. You must love not only the proposed end, but the means as well, because it is going to be a long, difficult journey with an uncertain payoff.

Developing Zealous Confidence

Among the ingredients to support the successful realization of your vision is the determination to see it through. It is often an entrepreneur's lack of determination that causes a venture-in-the-making to falter. Increasing the level of confidence you have in yourself and your vision can bolster determination.

> **Once you have established a vision and you have confidence and belief, there is no such thing as failure. There is only quitting.**

Knowledge creates belief and belief creates confidence. Therefore, you might reason that confidence comes from knowing your subject well and knowing how to advance it—and this must come from learning and experience. Get that first! Motivation comes from the burning desire to make a difference.

Once you have established a vision and you have confidence and belief, there is no such thing as failure. There is only quitting. Therefore the ultimate entrepreneurial trait is tenacity. You must stick to your vision and your venture no matter how tough it gets.

When to Take the Plunge

Since we have been talking about entrepreneurial traits, it is worth mentioning the initial step for first-time entrepreneurs, especially for those established in "safe" jobs. That first formidable step is knowing when to take the plunge from the security of a regular paycheck into a venture where you may not know when the next check is coming.

Working for someone else does hold appeal. There are perks like paid vacations, health care policies, a paycheck that increases by 6 percent every year and a half—if you're lucky—with nicely packaged retirement benefits. But lurking in the shadows of employment are things they never tell you when you're hired on. Your company doesn't talk about the downsizing that might take your job. Nor will they tell you that your ideas, vision, and passion will be strangled by bureaucracy, or even better yet, fear. And best of all, they may lead you to believe that the comfort of the old boy network is a valid remuneration for the yes-man behavior they expect.

These conditions are not tolerable to the rising entrepreneur, but leaving the comfort of a steady paycheck is not easy. Fear of failure and going bankrupt can be formidable diversions. Spouses, children, mortgages, car payments, and fear of the unknown can all be reasons people hesitate in their decision to become an entrepreneur. Almost every entrepreneur experiences these hesitations before making his or her final decision. And it is not a decision to be taken lightly.

I left a job as an engineer at Westinghouse to start ConQuest Software. I had no guarantee of success. At the time, I had a secure paycheck, two children to raise, and a mortgage to pay. The only assurance concerning the future endeavor was a letter of commitment from the first customer for a $50,000 order. I built confidence by carefully planning this venture. And I was willing to put in $50,000 while my partner chipped in $20,000 to make it succeed. I built up additional confidence by reading self-help books like *Think and Grow Rich* (which I highly recommend). In short order, we landed a $30,000 consulting contract to help keep us going and grow ConQuest to a million-dollar company that was sold to Excalibur in 1990 for $33 million.

The truth is, in the beginning you never know if a new venture will succeed. You have to be willing to give it a shot; otherwise, you will be a prisoner of your own fear. Building confidence is an important step. Doubt and uncertainty are the enemy. You cannot overcome fear with only one foot in the door. If you are working a full-time job and trying to raise money for a venture, you won't get your ideas off the ground. You need to show commitment to yourself and to the venture by working at it full time.

Carefully choose your time to embark on your entrepreneurial journey. While it may be unwise to keep working for someone else when you have what it takes to start a revolution, it would be equally unwise to pack your bags before you have a plan for yourself. Take a broad look at your life to see how a venture will fit in.

Building a venture takes many hours and relentless dedication, and can easily make you unbalanced if you do not work at it. New ventures are hard on family life and are known to have caused many divorces. The key to balancing your life between the venture and all the other aspects is to plan time for everything, but at the same time, stay focused on what is important and be flexible to make changes in your schedule if necessary. Jay Levinson, in *The Way of the Guerilla*, discusses new trends in the lifestyles of entrepreneurs, specifically focusing on the skills of achieving balance and working from home.

You need to ask yourself if, in the end, when you retire and are no longer energized, will you feel good about what you've accomplished in your career. If you are not yet convinced of your need to break free, and you do get satisfaction working for someone else, then stay with "the company." But if you know what you want and have confidence that you can achieve your goals, it's time for you to begin.

The Idea, the Vision, the Horizon

So what comes first? Is it the desire to be an entrepreneur or the idea for some great venture that causes you to decide to become one? There is no right answer to this question. Nothing is more important than having a vision and being driven to accomplish your goals. Everything flows from this motivation. If you already have an idea, then you are a step ahead. If you have decided that you want to be an entrepreneur but you don't have a billion-dollar idea yet, maybe it's just not the right time.

Inspiration is unpredictable. While it happens in its own time, there are some things you can do to cultivate your vision.

How do you come up with a brilliant idea and vision? As previously suggested, draw on your education, work experience, and market insights. Any one of these threads could be the key. But inspiration is unpredictable. While it happens in its own time, there are some things you can do to cultivate your vision in the following areas:

Educational Background

Have you mastered a technical trade at the graduate school level? Are you in touch with the current research in your field? Do you track the research programs at local universities and do you know the professors who are experts? If so, then drawing on this expertise is an excellent start toward a technologically driven business—but be very careful to validate the market need for what you are doing. If you have not yet mastered a technical trade, then maybe you should consider going back to school.

Work Experience

Have you worked in the field of your planned venture before? Are you aware of the current industry practices and the state of the art? Have you observed limitations that need to be overcome in order to provide an economic benefit? If so, then your work experience may be an excellent source for tapping into ideas for the next venture. If you answered no to more than one of the above questions, then perhaps you should consider more practical experience.

Recognition of a Market Need

Recognizing a market need may occur to you while you're still on the other side of the fence, i.e. the consumer side. Perhaps you have been a frustrated customer before. Perhaps you were not able to find the service or product you needed for your work or home life. Or perhaps you have worked in customer service and you have observed customers in need of something that was unavailable. Such experiences are excellent sources of venture ideas because they are driven by market needs.

Admiring the success of others is inspirational. Reading about and spending time with entrepreneurs is perhaps the single most motivating experience for anyone wishing to pursue a venture. Take a look at *Microcosm* by George Gilder for a behind-the-scenes look at the rising of the early computer industry. The astounding accomplishments of others within the computer field provide strong inspiration for any would-be entrepreneur. Or, consider working for an entrepreneur to inspire your own entrepreneurial vision. You'll benefit by learning from others without shouldering the burden yourself. The entrepreneur will benefit from your drive and enthusiasm.

Another way to look for venture ideas is to recognize and exploit macro trends occurring today. For example, Peter Drucker writes about the current transformation from an industrial society to a knowledge society in his book *Post Capitalist Society*. This book was written before the commercialization of the Internet, but its deep insights are valuable in determining how to position a venture within a new trend in our future society. A knowledge society will be very different from the industrialized societies of the past. Increasing emphasis will be placed on services, knowledge, and access to information, and decreasing emphasis will be placed on manual labor, manufacturing, and capital-intense heavy industry. All of these trends can be fruitful areas for innovation to arise.

Perhaps a slightly more exciting read, *The Long Boom* provides insight in pointing out the broad trends that are expected to be hot in the near future. Any venture that plays a role within one of these trends is bound to encounter success to some degree. Peter Schwartz, et al, defines the "Long Boom" as the unprecedented global growth that the world is currently undergoing. He expects this boom to last about twenty-five years, despite the near recession of 2001 and the bursting of the Internet bubble. Some key trends and Schwartz's thoughts about them are outlined below.

Once you have established an idea for your venture, it is extremely important to look at how you ultimately want your business to grow. You must not establish a me-too venture or a variation of something that already exists. Rather, you must determine in which direction the world is headed and then get there first. In order to determine where you are today, or where you must start, it is imperative that you establish a long-range goal for your venture.

Key Technology Trends of the Long Boom

In their groundbreaking book, *The Long Boom*, Peter Schwartz and Peter Leydon identify key technological trends shaping the next twenty years or more. These trends are emerging in areas that entrepreneurs should look toward for innovative ideas. The most significant trends are summarized below:

- Personal Computer: Computer and telecommunication technologies are creating a fundamentally new infrastructure upon which our twenty-first-century world will be based.
- Globalization: The growing global economy will lead to the increasing population of the new global middle class—well-off people who share certain values that transcend borders. This new middle class promises to be a force pushing for widespread changes, including greater democratic control of all aspects of the economy and society.

- Biotech and Genomics: The next technological wave that we will all ride is biotechnology, and this one will blow your mind. By the year 2020, biotechnology will bring more change to the human species than we have experienced in the last million years.
- Nanotechnology and the Environment: We're going to be able to construct products atom by atom, very quickly, through billions of simultaneous actions, with no waste—it will be kind of like having an atomic Lego set that will ultimately make anything and everything.
- Alternative Energy Sources: In recent years, the fuel cell has been making a comeback after a series of technological improvements brought the cost down.
- Expanding into Space: The next great breakthroughs concerning space exploration will initially boggle us. These discoveries will then profoundly affect us. And eventually, we'll take them for granted.

When developing the ultimate vision of your business, you must begin with where the market is today and clearly identify what market need you are fulfilling. This step of the process cannot be underestimated. There are too many cool technologies searching for a market. It's a very tough place to be! It is important to decide who you are, and who you are not, and stick to your focus, avoiding the temptation to chase every moving target with dollar signs on it.

From your vision you can develop a strategic architecture for your venture. This will serve as a kind of conceptual road map that shows where the idea for your venture stands today and how that idea will evolve over time. You will need crystal clear clarity when it comes to this vision and strategic architecture. Without these two tools, you will not be able to communicate your venture's objective, your excitement, and your passion to your prospects, employees, and stakeholders.

The bottom line is, you have to figure out where the market is going and get there first. And you must do this in a field in which you have the knowledge, experience, inspiration, belief, confidence, and above all, the passion needed to succeed. If you wish to have a more methodical approach to finding your idea, James Cook in *The Start-Up Entrepreneur* devotes a chapter to ways of finding a business—but your idea still needs to come from your own personal vision, your passion, and your skills.

Testing the Idea

Great ideas and great visions only deserve to be called great if your target customer thinks so too. After all, the only absolute requirement to make a business a real business is a customer. Therefore, the sickeningly practical dog food analogy is the best acid test of your venture: Are the dogs eating the dog food? Or at this conceptual stage, will the dogs eat the dog food? The former is the acid test of the venture; the latter is your self-test before you are ready for funding.

> **Great ideas and great visions only deserve to be called great if your target customer thinks so too.**

The best way to pass this test is by understanding your customers' needs. There is really no substitute for you, the entrepreneur, going out to meet your customers and prospects. Ask them if they would buy your hypothetical product or invest in your service. If they say no, then ask them why not. Let the customers be a part of the design process and secure their loyalty while you're at it. At this early stage, however, the only way to test your idea is to talk and sell conceptually. Listen carefully to what your prospective customers have to say. Humble yourself and keep your zealous optimism in check.

Flexibility is needed if the market tells you your vision is not viable. Sales, rather than technology, will drive your venture—make no mistake about it. Early on, you need to interview future customers to find out what their product wishes are and test to see whether or not they would buy what you plan to build. However, after the initial stages of your product development, your involvement with customers is far from over. You need to keep customers involved as you design and evolve your product or service. This task can be accomplished through ongoing dialogue with your early adopter customers. These special customers are often very different from the mainstream customers you will need to create a true growth venture. They are technology enthusiasts who are driven by a love of new things; attracting their enthusiasm is a must for a high-tech venture. Your sales into this segment will sustain the company while you shift your sales focus to larger, mainstream customers. Geoffrey Moore in *Crossing the Chasm* explores this concept in great depth—it is a must-read and a classic for entrepreneurs involved in high-tech ventures.

Sometimes you can obtain valuable feedback by running focus groups for potential users of your product. These sessions will aid you in both learning how the general public perceives your current product and discovering your users' needs. However, focus groups do not often give you great insight into the future. The users who attend focus groups live in the present and hold practical, everyday jobs. Often, when a technology breakthrough is involved, your prospective customer will not yet know that he needs your planned product. How, then, do you test the market in this situation?

There is no substitute for street smarts. It is in this area that your confidence, knowledge, and leadership really shine through. Spend lots of time talking with your prospects, not in your head. Sniff around for competition. You don't want to be the leader of a me-too venture whose company dies a slow death. Thoroughly researching your competition can provide important insights and can also help you avoid positioning mistakes. The best way to find out about potential competitors is by attending trade shows in your industry where these vendors are likely to exhibit their products.

No amount of market research, sniffing, competitive evaluation, or any other form of market study will assure your success. These assessments can help you to maximize your chances, make life easier, or get you off to a faster start. But in the end, it is you who has to execute and you who has to hang in there when the going gets tough.

Chapter 2

Founding the Team

"The important thing to recognize is that it takes a team, and the team ought to get credit for the wins and the losses. Successes have many fathers, failures have none."
—Philip Caldwell

One of the key themes in this book is the idea that building powerful teams is essential to the success of a venture. Both initial and extended teams are vitally important in the process of launching your vision. This chapter will explore the issues involved in selecting your founding team, advisors, and early hires. It will also discuss how to motivate and integrate your team from the start so that your venture will be driven forward powerfully and effectively.

Selling Your Vision

To build a founding team you must sell the vision you have developed for your venture. Doing so is paramount to attracting and recruiting any resource you need, including potential customers, funding sources, and other resources necessary to accomplish the mission of the venture.

Selling your vision requires charisma and a personality that attracts others like a magnet. These qualities are brought about by your enthusiasm, confidence, interest in other people, knowledge of your subject, and, above all, your passion.

The key to attracting a strong founding group is in being able to communicate your vision in a manner that excites others. The vision must be one that others can believe in and take ownership of as they assist you in making the venture a success. When Powerize.com was founded, our vision was for a "single source access to information." The information Powerize.com users could access was a combination of professional online services, the Internet, and enterprise data in the Intranet. The "Powerize Server" was capable of searching, filtering, organizing, and rendering customized XML (a standard Internet markup language) on the fly from all of these sources simultaneously. This vision attracted a staff of ten talented people from day one. Whether ten was the right number to start with will be discussed later. But the vision is what initially attracted the team and bound us together as we strived to succeed in a common mission.

The key to attracting a strong founding group is to have a compelling vision—one that others can believe in and take ownership of...

Michael Lewis in *The New New Thing* describes legendary Silicon Valley entrepreneur Jim Clark, who founded Silicon Graphics, Netscape, and Healtheon/WebMD. Clark has achieved an almost iconic following due to his reputation as a revolutionary and his unmatched record of success. While it seems quite certain that his vision attracted the teams for Silicon Graphics and Netscape, it may be that his name alone did it for Healtheon. Interestingly, Clark never went to work for Healtheon—he just founded it using his name and venture capital, which he obtained using a diagram drawn on the back of a napkin. Don't count on doing that!

At Silicon Graphics, the ultimate vision was to create the best server for graphics, and eventually for the entire entertainment industry. The company's engineers rapidly pursued the cutting-edge technology. Silicon Graphics was truly a technology-driven company. Their focus made them attractive initially, but was also most likely what caused their downfall. Ultimately, low-end competitors, i.e. Microsoft, started nipping away at their market share. To defend against this kind of attack, the vision needed to be expanded to attain a niche market that it could have owned.

Netscape's original vision was to have an icon on every desktop in the world. With the commercial introduction of the Internet browser, Netscape changed the way of the desktop by becoming a severe threat to Microsoft's domination of this market. Microsoft's marketing muscle ultimately won out, but not before Netscape sold out for $4B in stock to America Online. Netscape is widely viewed as the company that put the Internet on the map for the general public.

Powerful visions attract people, money, customers, press attention, investment bankers, and help win market share. Very few ventures will have the revolutionary vision of Netscape or the luck of Netscape's timing, but even a spark can go a long way. The excitement of your vision can make an impact and attract people who have the desire to be part of something that will ultimately change the world.

Sometimes a vision may initially appear sexy but proves incomplete or incoherent with a little more digging. Although this lack of a clearly defined vision may not seem like a problem in the beginning, it will eventually affect the company's success. For example, in 1995 ConQuest merged with Excalibur Technologies. Like ConQuest, Excalibur was a very small company. But Excalibur had a strong banker behind it—Allen & Company in New York. Excalibur had been hyped as a company with glitzy technology for retrieving multimedia information. After it merged with ConQuest, the new company had four different products that served essentially three to four different markets. Excalibur was still promoting its technology image, while its business strategy was very opportunistic and was driven by quarterly revenue targets rather than a strategic mission. Company management's preoccupation with Wall Street and the opinions of its investment bankers drew the focus away from its core strategy. This focus on short-term results stole significant energy from the execution of the company's total vision.

In a scenario like this, a company is apt to do well in good times, when Wall Street values technology stories, but not so well in down markets, when quarterly performance is jagged due to a wandering strategy. In fact, in a six-year period after the merger, the stock price of Excalibur (now Convera, Nasdaq:CNVR) went from $15 to $39 to $4 to $68 and back to $2. Had the company focused its strategy on serving the Internet market in 1995, rather than attempting to serve all markets, it may have done significantly better (but it still would have crashed with the market). On the other hand, if it had focused on another market, such as the enterprise market, it may have performed in a more stable manner. Despite this story of ups and downs, Convera is still a promising company with strong backing and it possesses the potential to soar again. Indeed, it should, if it can achieve clarity of vision.

How do you sell your vision to gain valuable connections and, most importantly, a founding team? You do so by living and breathing your vision and maintaining a naturally enthusiastic, knowledgeable, confident, and passionate attitude. You must know your message, be absolutely clear about who you are, and doggedly stick to it. In closing this section, a few suggestions about how to sell your vision can be found in the table below.

How to Sell Your Vision

- Make sure it is a worthy vision—one in which people want to take part.
- Communicate the main focus of your vision in a simple, clear, and concise way.
- Do your homework: know everything there is to know about your vision.
- Believe in your vision and be totally confident that it can become a reality.
- Be organized: have a strategy, a plan, and a product or service.
- Understand the person to whom you are speaking and try to fulfill their needs.
- Don't be cocky, arrogant, or full of hyperbole—good visions will sell on their own.
- Let your passion shine through! If you are excited, others will be excited as well.

The Initial Team

Your initial team—the first three to six people—will have a profound influence on the future, culture, and tactical direction of your business. In the frenzy to establish your business, it is quite easy to forget just how strongly this early group will impact your company. Choose these people carefully. This section discusses some of the fundamental considerations in selecting, attracting, and organizing your initial team.

Size and Composition of the Founding Team

Every situation is different, but perhaps the ideal size for a founding group is three people. One person is clearly not enough—one person is not a company. However, starting with too large a group can be a team-building challenge and a distraction from early work.

The founding group you establish may work together for several months or longer, planning a venture before the launch occurs. At the time of the launch, you may recruit more people to work for your company, but these people will not be the initial founders. The founding group defines the company and completes the early groundbreaking work before adding the rest of the staff.

Every situation is different, but perhaps the ideal size for a founding group is three people.

What kind of people do you need to start a company? It depends on the nature of the venture and the stage of the company. For discussion's sake, we will consider the founding of the company and the launch as two separate events. Founding takes place when two to four people get together and decide to develop a venture. They work together for several months, some part time and some full time and eventually more than full time. At this stage, the venture is being defined and developed. The launch takes place after the founding, when the early start-up team is being recruited. At this time, you may choose to add another three to five people to your company, but again, this decision will depend upon each individual situation.

The important issue of roles and positions will need to be addressed early in the process. Sometimes technical people collaborate to build a product and start a high-tech venture knowing that they will recruit professional management. Such managers are not usually members of the technical founding team. Other times they are and must then decide which roles to play.

The table below outlines key positions that are needed at the outset, as well as positions that can be deferred until a later date.

POSITION	FOUNDING TEAM COMPOSITION
CEO Chief Executive Officer	The founding team needs to be very clear about who is in charge. This person may or may not be the long-term CEO, but at the start, this person is acting as the CEO.
COO Chief Operating Officer	The choice as to whether or not to have a COO on the founding team depends upon your team's makeup and needs. The CEO could serve in this role as well and make a COO unnecessary.
CTO Chief Technology Officer	In a high-tech venture, a CTO, or a "technical head honcho" is needed at the beginning. Engineers have a *de facto* pecking order and a need to respect their leader in a technical manner.
CFO Chief Financial Officer	Normally, a CFO is unnecessary until later in the venture. A controller is needed at this time only if there are numerous transactions being made. A part-time accountant can usually serve the need.
VP Business Development	If business deals or strategic alliances are to be formed right away, this position needs to be covered. However, it may be the CEO or COO that does this job.
Sales Force	Unless you have a completed product, you do not need a sales force yet. Early conceptual selling should be done by the founders until you have a proven product.
Engineers	Engineers are needed right from the beginning. It is a huge mistake to found a high-tech company without at least one engineer on the founding team.
Admin Staff	You may or may not need administrative support during the first few months. Normally, the administrative staff is not considered to be part of the core founding team.

Picking the Founders and Early Team

So how do you pick and recruit your founding team and early staff? There are no magic formulas. Perhaps your personal network combined with enthusiasm, charisma, and the strength of your vision will do it. But many first-time entrepreneurs do not yet have a strong network. So where do you look and whom do you pick? Sometimes it's easier to talk about what *not* to do, rather than what to do. Let's start with some examples of issues that have cropped up as a result of inadequate positioning.

My second venture, Powerize.com, was launched at a time when money was freely available and everything dot-com was in a royal hurry to "get there first." Given this environment, I made the same mistake everyone else starting a venture in 1997 made—I went too fast and built the team too rapidly, not allowing enough time for it to become smoothly integrated.

Powerize.com started with nine people—too many people to develop team dynamics. The vision for the company was to aggregate business information and create personalized publications that would synthesize the results of many searches. Most of the early staff was composed of engineers. Aside from establishing an overly large founding team, I made a mistake in not appointing a CTO right from the start. I put everyone together in a creative design pool and expected the natural chief to emerge. Instead of following this plan, the situation led to fighting among the engineers. One very intelligent engineer had to be fired because he was stubborn about taking an approach different from that of the other engineers. As the company grew, a major battle for technical leadership arose amongst our two product leaders. This political battleground was never fully settled before the company was sold, and we lost countless hours of productivity over it.

Always have a CTO on your founding team.

Powerize.com had an early product deadline so it would be ready for Fall Internet World in New York in late 1997. While this deadline served as a group milestone that gave us a focus for an enormous amount of work, it proved to be more than our small team could handle. In an attempt to better cope with our deadlines, we hired the Adrenaline Group, a Web design company in Washington, D.C. The guys at Adrenaline were technically brilliant and very headstrong. We made our product goal, but the resulting design deviated from our original vision. In order to make the deadline, simplifications were made that included leaving out the feature that was most vital to our vision—personalized publication. This exclusion had a price that would be paid for many months to come.

Both of these mistakes—expecting the emergence of a natural leader and simplifying our product solely for the purpose of meeting deadlines— could have been avoided if we had a good, solid CTO on the starting team. While Powerize.com turned out to be a successful business venture, it was a nightmare managing engineering. Having the leadership from the beginning would have prevented the internal struggle for control and focused our efforts so that Adrenaline would not have pulled us off course. Lesson learned: always, always have a well-qualified CTO on your founding team.

Professional sales teams are good at selling mature, perfected products, but entrepreneurial teams and the founding group are best for the early-stage conceptual selling.

To expand on the previous table, there are some positions that are not needed from the start. I would advise against a CFO or VP Sales if your venture is a seed stage venture. The CFO can wait, unless he or she is integrally involved in the start-up in other ways. Usually the CFO contributes immensely to a later stage venture, but does not add value relative to cost in the seed stages. Use a part-time accountant until you have an established business.

Similarly for the VP Sales and the sales force. These people are also highly talented and immensely valuable to a venture with a mature product. But most are not equipped to sell early stage technology before it is packaged for the mainstream market.

When ConQuest released its search engine product in 1992, I hired three experienced software sales people, including a VP, as the initial sales team. For the next eighteen months, we did about $2.5M in revenue. I personally made over 90 percent of the sales. This was very frustrating for both the sales team and me. Eventually, after two years and some turnover in management, the sales team began to make substantial sales.

The biggest lesson I learned from this experience is that professional sales teams are good at selling mature, perfected products, but entrepreneurial teams and the founding group are best for the early stage conceptual selling. The reason: at this early stage, the success in selling comes from selling the vision, not the product. The product is not yet mature enough to attract mainstream buyers.

Finding Prospects

The founding team has a profound influence on the success and the culture of the venture. It's a network of close partnerships that lasts a long time. Pick these people carefully! Where do you look for prospects? Look to former co-workers, fellow students or professors, local universities, networking groups, referrals from your associates, etc. Referrals are many times the best source—they come with someone's vote of confidence, precluding the dreaded task of doing background checks on possible candidates.

The people who can help you the most at this early stage are those who possess the skills necessary to address your specific needs; a team attitude; and a tolerance for risk, uncertainty, and doubt. You want self-starters, not people who need a lot of coddling and training.

How about your friends? Should you have friends or neighbors as a part of the founding team? It's done all the time but it's not always a good idea. Tread very carefully with this one! Working with a friend or neighbor has the obvious advantage of knowing what you are getting. However, there are several disadvantages, including the possibility of broken friendships, venture capitalists looking down upon you for choosing your friends, and the possibility that you judge your friends only through rose-colored glasses. The bottom line: hire friends and neighbors only when it is justified on the basis of the person's skill and only after you have had an open discussion about your friendship and business becoming mixed.

While at ConQuest, I hired an old buddy from a former job—an ex-Air Force pilot with excellent interpersonal skills. He was originally in marketing at an aerospace firm, but he had retired and was looking for a new opportunity. I hired him to sell software. As it turned out, he was not computer literate enough to be credible. He went from an environment where he was very well respected to one in which he struggled. I eventually had to let him go. This was extremely difficult due to our friendship, but it was something that had to be done. If you are thinking about hiring a close friend, you need to carefully consider whether or not it could end in a similar way.

The founding team has a profound influence on the success and the culture of the venture. It's a close partnership that lasts a long time.

Also, while it may be attractive to go with some part-timers, be very cautious when hiring them. Many of these part-time workers will never join your firm and it will be difficult to redeem the stock they were awarded upon hire. I had an experience with a venture where one of the founders flat-out refused to quit his full-time job, even when the firm needed him the most. Eventually, the founding team had to oust him and negotiate a drastic reduction in his equity. Fortunately, it was a happy ending, but it could have been quite onerous.

Exceptions to the Rule

At some point your intuition may lead you astray and you will break these rules in selecting your founding team. When I founded Powerize.com, I recruited my next door neighbor, Mark, to be the company COO. Not only did I do that, but I also agreed to allow him to work for his other employer for a year before joining Powerize.com full time. This situation violates three rules right off the bat: 1) don't go in business your friends, 2) you don't need a COO right away, and 3) make sure all of the founders quit their old jobs before joining. However, in this special case, I was very familiar with Mark's skills and they complemented mine. I am a blue sky visionary and Mark is a detail-oriented operational manager. I knew I would have to spend most of my time raising money and I needed someone I trusted to run the company once our product was released. It worked out very well. Mark was both a top-notch operational manager as well as a natural entrepreneur. This scenario, however, is the exception and not the rule for how to found a team.

ConQuest, on the other hand, started out very differently from Powerize.com. It began with only two people—Paul Nelson as the CTO and lead developer and myself as the visionary. Not only did we start out by subleasing an office in a mattress factory, but we also worked alone for an entire year before the technical team was recruited. We eventually recruited three excellent programmers—all of whom agreed to work only for stock for at least a year. This arrangement does not work during all economic times (notably, not in the dot-com era, but maybe again since the Internet bubble has burst). However, it worked well for us then, and we continued the practice on a 50 percent pay and 50 percent stock basis for at least another year before we had a normal payroll. In the end, it paid off for all of them. Our programmers each became millionaires or multi-millionaires. But they weren't in it for the monetary gain—they wanted the technical challenge and the excitement of being part of something new. Clearly, the initial vision was compelling and Paul and I recruited the right people to bring our venture to reality.

One last consideration: it is important that you give any partnership a trial period before making a permanent decision. If the partnership does not initially work, it would probably be best if you parted ways before the start of the venture. In this case, if you are the owner of the intellectual property, you should insure the exclusive right to keep the ownership.

Motivating Others

Once your team has been assembled, its members must be highly motivated to execute the business. The founders have built-in motivation—it's their company. They invented it. The first round of staff is often considered a group of founders as well. These people join to be a part of something that will change the world. One of the keys to your venture's success lies in keeping your recruits motivated and energized. This section discusses how to motivate people by allowing them to have an impact on the vision and make a difference through their work, equity participation, and the overall sense of the team's well-being.

The CEO's Charisma

While there are many methods that can be used to motivate and excite your initial team, this task is ultimately in your hands and in the way you project your enthusiasm and charisma. If you are the principal founder, so much of the venture and culture is defined by who you are—like it or not.

Consider, for example, a small start-up in Pennsylvania called Infonautics that was founded in the early nineties. This company delivered online information to K to 12 students to help them with their homework. Originally called Homework Helper, this service debuted on Prodigy before widespread use of the Internet. Everyone in the industry knew the founder, Marvin Weinberger. He was enthusiastic, prolific, and stubborn, and he was widely known as "Marvelous Marvin." Whenever anyone walked in the doors of Infonautics, they were immediately lavished with food—sodas, candy bars, fruit, cookies, etc. They were made to feel at home. This set-up was a product of Marvin's imagination, as was the company. Everybody liked Marvin. His success was partially driven by his kamikaze personality. His managerial style can best be understood by a skydiving analogy: Marvin jumps out of an airplane before his parachute is completely ready and then asks everyone else to follow. Marvin's commitment, despite his eccentricity, is what drew others to work for him. They believed in his vision. Indeed, it was his eccentricity and tenacity that drove Infonautics forward in tough times. Marvin succeeded at getting Information Technology (IT) services work from a system integrator and paid his rent in stock.

There are also many legendary Silicon Valley ventures known by the personalities of their founders. Consider Apple Computer and Steve Jobs, Microsoft and Bill Gates, Oracle and Larry Ellison. Almost everyone has read about these founding CEOs. Not every start-up will have a legendary founder, but who you are and how you conduct yourself will most definitely be a significant motivating or de-motivating force for your team.

While there are many methods that can be used to motivate and excite your early team, this task is ultimately in your hands and in the way you project your enthusiasm and charisma.

Your personality can work against you if you have the wrong attitude. I once met an entrepreneur from the Mid-Atlantic region who owned a neural net company. This person had put $250,000 of his own money into his company and he had a couple of part-time junior programmers working for him. He oozed arrogance and did not listen to anyone's input. He owned over 90 percent of his company and was seeking to raise $2M of venture capital for which he was willing to give up only 15 percent of his company. He couldn't understand why the venture capitalists weren't lined up to fund him.

The neural net market did not flourish and I don't know what happened to his company. However, I do know that he made many mistakes. Because of his arrogance, unyielding attitude, and refusal to share equity, he did not attract a strong team. He did not value other viewpoints and had no charisma whatsoever. He was downright abrasive. And on top of all this, he was outlandishly unrealistic about how much equity he would have to sell for venture capital.

This example illustrates that your charisma and personality are absolutely vital to the potential success of your venture and can work to support or undermine your efforts depending upon how you choose to use them.

Building a "Shared Vision"

Peter Senge, in *The Fifth Discipline*, describes a concept called "shared vision." Senge spends a great deal of time explaining how to achieve a shared vision. Although your venture is founded on *your* vision, it ultimately needs to be built on the *shared* vision of your founding team and early staff. It is vitally important to include your team in further defining and refining the vision. You can start with your vision but it must evolve into a team vision that encourages participation from your staff. Creating an atmosphere of involvement where contributions are valued imbues employees with a sense of ownership.

Managing and coordinating a team is an ongoing process. Regular time needs to be set aside for team building and reaching a shared vision. We set aside time for these important discussions at ConQuest with the help of a professional coach. We felt that it would be beneficial to seek outside help because we changed our revenue model quickly from a direct, whole-product sales approach to an indirect, OEM (Original Equipment Manufacturer) approach. We ultimately lost the enthusiasm of a couple members of the management team but retained the focus and commitment of our core support staff.

It is not always possible to build a shared vision in which 100 percent of the staff agrees on the direction it will take. Sometimes, there will be people who don't agree with the strategic direction of the company. When this happens, there is no choice but to part ways. A small venture cannot afford to have people pulling in different directions, wasting resources, and disrupting the culture.

Technology vs. Sales People

Everyone, not just the founder, must play a role in ensuring that appropriate motivational appeals are applied. Technology and sales people are often motivated by different rewards. Technically minded engineers have the desire to build or create something and make a difference. This sense of ingenuity is more important to them than money. Equity is an important motivational tool to them as well, although less so than the need to build something new. They are creating the product for a company that needs it to succeed and they should therefore be rewarded for that. Closing a deal and reaping instant rewards, on the other hand, motivates sales people. Making or beating quota is a real high for them. Their income needs to be directly proportional to their success. Sales commissions are generally more important than stock to this group of people.

Keeping both your technology and sales personnel motivated extends beyond rewards. You will also need to be sensitive to each group's fundamental character and not quash their spirit. Conflicts of interest will always arise. Your sales people will want to promise everything the customers asks and the technology people want to build and grow their product at a sane pace, without being told what to do by sales people. This conflict occurs in every venture and it requires a certain amount of managerial finesse. Sales people should be allowed to sell only what you have completed and tested. Engineers should take direction from corporate management or product management, but product development shouldn't veer off course for every customer or potential customer.

Distributing Equity

All employees in a venture should share in the stock option plan. It is important that everyone working for you feels that the company is "their" company. However, not all employees should share in founders' equity. The adjacent sidebar discusses the distribution of ownership in a start-up company.

Distributing Equity in a Start-Up Venture

How should equity be divided in a new venture? The process is an art, not a science. There are, however, some common sense principles that apply to this task.

It is generally a bad idea to have outsiders—especially those who have not invested cash in the company—hold large ownership stakes. Such a set-up demoralizes employees who have smaller stakes and sometimes leads to conflicts within the company. It can also be demoralizing if ownership is not distributed equitably. Employees understand cash investments, but they have difficulty with founder shares or options that are awarded to some people whose contributions do not appear to be commensurate to others.

It is useful to classify equity in three categories for an early stage company. There are founder shares, investor shares, and employee shares. Each type of share is classified differently, so we shall take them one step at a time. This is true whether you begin with a C-Corporation, S-Corporation, or LLC.

To determine the total number of shares, companies will often reverse from a hypothetical IPO. For example, you may assume that when the company goes public, you will have 10 million shares, of which the public owns 3 million. That means you have 7 million immediately prior to the IPO, the majority of which would have been allocated in multiple rounds of financing. Perhaps 30 percent or 3 million will go to the founders, management team, and employees. Founders may then start off by allocating 2 million shares and reserving 1 million for employees and management.

Founder Shares—These shares, which are typically common stock, go primarily to the two to four persons who found the company. The distribution may or may not be equal, depending upon your agreements and contributions, as well as who had the initial idea and intellectual capital to put the idea into action. A small amount (10 to 15 percent) of the founder shares may go to secondary team players, such as part-timers that will join you later. It is not a good idea for one single founder to own a majority, such as 70 percent or more, of the founder shares. This remarkably uneven distribution can upset other founders and it does not demonstrate team spirit at all.

Employee Shares—All employees in the early stages of a venture should share in the ownership of the company. Typically, their claim is made through stock option plans, both qualified and unqualified. Often equity is distributed after the company has a value. The vast majority of these shares go to the top two to four management slots, other than the founders. The remaining balance is split into pools for employees based upon level and time of entry. For example, if you allocate 1 million shares for the employees, you may reserve 600,000 for the top three management slots and 400,000 for all others.

Investor Shares—Normally, investor shares are preferred stock, determined in each round by the company valuation, which is usually set by the investor. Sometimes, early rounds including friends and family have valuations set by management. This is okay provided that these shares are not overpriced, which could lead to future difficulties in raising money.

The numerical examples above are provided for illustrative purposes. In the end, your accountants and lawyers will work out the distribution, with a high level of input from you. Your distribution may end up being very similar or somewhat different than those suggested here.

Managing to Achieve Goals

The company's vision provides guideposts for an energetic staff that is working toward a common goal. These guideposts, along with the incentives you provide, may be enough to keep everyone coming to work each day and making positive progress. But some situations require stringent management. Managing a diverse employee base takes a special blend of skills. You can't simply bark orders. You will find that certain people need to conclude for themselves what to do. Your job is only to ensure that they conclude what you want them to yet believe that it was their own decision.

Consider a situation I encountered with the engineers at ConQuest. We had a particularly talented bunch of engineers who occasionally had slightly jaundiced attitude. They looked askance at management as if anyone who was not an engineer was a second-class citizen. As a recovering engineer, I can attest to this attitude. However, it does present some problems in working towards goals. I noticed that our engineers at ConQuest had a high regard for any customer who was paying us money. Not surprising. I also found that one of the best ways to get our engineering staff to perform a task quickly and efficiently was to go to one of our customers they regarded highly and ask them to request it! I used this technique time and again very successfully and the engineers never knew I was managing them at all. At first I found it infuriating that I had to go through customers to get them to do what needed to be done, but eventually I accepted it as a cultural nuance, indeed one that worked very well.

Sometimes, an agreed upon team goal serves to focus the staff in a very effective manner. Again at ConQuest, in 1993, the marketing group wanted to go to the AIIM show (Association of Imaging Information Management) in Chicago at McCormick Center. While this show was not a perfect fit for our product, I decided to take it on for a different reason. We announced that AIIM '93 would be our product debut. This imminent event immediately drove a stake into the ground and caused our engineers to complete the product, our marketing staff to refine our collateral materials and pricing strategy, and our sales team to organize an initial campaign, all before the scheduled date of the AIIM show. This event did more for internal management than it did for our market penetration. It sparked a tremendous confluence of energy that saved our company three to six months in calendar time. This technique was so successful that I used it again when Powerize.com was founded, by announcing a product launch at the New York Fall Internet World in late 1997.

Selecting Your Advisors

One of the challenges of starting a venture is to create the appearance and firepower of a venture that is "larger than life." This gets you off to a faster start because it helps build momentum in your venture. One of the most valuable ways to multiply your firepower is to build a strong network of advisors. Advisors, provided that they are well chosen, can provide you with valuable advice and extensive networks and add to your credibility. It is truly a shame to find a stubborn entrepreneur who is otherwise an extremely talented individual but is unwilling to enlist or heed advisors.

> **One of the most valuable ways to multiply your firepower is to build a strong network of advisors.**

Choosing the right advisors can add to your venture by sharpening your strategy, strengthening your management team, further motivating your team, and providing leads and contacts to secure customers and financing. Picking the wrong advisors may not only be costly, but draining as well.

Advisors can be informal contacts, directors on your board, or appointees to a formal advisory board. It is up to you how you want to arrange their affiliation. How should you go about selecting your advisors? First, you need people who are well known in your industry and have a strong network of connections. This will help you to associate with those who are important in your field and, at the same time, it will add credibility to your business. You may also need advisors who have business knowledge that you don't. It is helpful to have someone with strong financial connections. Having an angel investor or an experienced entrepreneur as an advisor isn't a bad idea either. These people will be able to relate to the experiences of first starting a company. In addition, they often have free time and the desire to contribute to other start-up companies. Furthermore, they can be a very competent source of creative thought.

Do a little bit of homework before making any permanent decisions about your advisors. In 1991, I met Don Wilson, founding president of Mead Data Central and an accomplished venture manager as well. We met at the Information Industry Association where I learned that he was one of the most active and well-respected people in the industry. As a result of what I learned about him at the IIA, I recruited him as Chairman of the Board for ConQuest. He served us well with an extensive network of contacts and a deep understanding of the industry.

Not performing an extensive background check can cost you valuable time and money when launching your venture. This proved to be true with one of my first business lawyers. I initially hired him because he agreed to work the first fifteen hours for free and then at a reduced rate. The lawyer got overloaded with his work and couldn't keep up with even the smallest jobs that we assigned to him. After some digging we learned that he had been withholding information from us. He had been fired by his firm and didn't tell us. We quickly changed firms. Had I done a proper investigation up front, I might have decided against the unknown lawyer with free service and gone with someone carrying a stronger reputation, even if he charged for his labor.

In another similar blunder, I met a fellow who claimed to be a former top sales executive for one of the largest software companies. Let's call him Harry. Harry was charismatic and had quite a few business connections. I was in a hurry so I did not call references. Harry was hard-working and had a good heart, but he also had a political agenda. He wasn't performing his selling duties in a completely devoted manner because he placed more importance on trying to gain control and influence in the office. And it turned out he was viewed negatively by the customers as sort of a cracker-jack salesman. Harry often sold the customers products we didn't have and this situation put our engineers in a tailspin. He was used to selling a "what you see is what you get" kind of product as opposed to the consultative sell of a complex product. When we finally parted ways, we got ourselves involved in a legal tussle. A bit of a background check turned up the fact that he was fired from both of his previous software executive jobs, and as a result he had sued the companies. Had I done a thorough background check, I may not have hired him.

Indeed, always check out the reputations of any potential advisors before hiring them. You do not want to affiliate with someone who is not respected in your industry. Nor do you want to pay large fees and not receive the value you need at the time. Also, watch out for high-priced consultants. Cash grabbers are a red flag in a venture—you cannot afford to be paying large per diem fees for these advisors. If they correctly understand the game, they will do the job mostly for equity. As for those advisors who are trying to make a living off of working for your company, you'd be better off without them. You should not feel obligated to put everyone you hire on your board of directors. Many of them will not even want to be on your board. Overall, you are just looking for a few good people who can give you leverage and are willing to work on your terms.

Using Incubators

Another potentially effective way to extend the power of your team is through the use of an incubator. An incubator is a service that can accelerate your business, provide real estate and money, give access to university resources, offer mentorship and business services, and, in some cases, develop business contacts. Incubators vary greatly. The word "incubator" got a bad reputation during the dot-com tidal wave because people tried to abuse the capital market and create IPO factories out of them. Not all incubators deserved this reputation, however. Perhaps the IPO factories did, but true business incubators perform a valuable service for certain kinds of companies.

Incubators can be both a blessing and a curse, and their possible uses for your venture depend upon your unique situation. The earliest incubators were real estate plays, essentially dividing a building into suites that didn't require long leases with a central reception area and conference room. While such ideas have merit, modern incubators offer many more amenities, including management services, mentorship, Internet service provision, and sometimes seed capital and a "keiretsu." These latter two items are the most valuable, but often come at a very expensive equity cost.

> **Among the most attractive benefits of the more modern "new economy" style incubators, aside from the availability of seed capital, is the notion of a "keiretsu."**

Beyond the obviously beneficial real estate aspects, one of the fundamental ideas of an incubator is to provide services for your business that are necessary evils, but not fundamental tasks that are on the mainstream path toward your horizon. Setting up an e-mail system, renting a copier, arranging travel services, negotiating a lease, developing a stock option plan, evaluating an accounting system, etc., are all examples of niceties that often come along with incubators. While such services can be very convenient, there is a certain stewardship or entrepreneurial grooming that you gain by handling these things yourself. Some venture capitalists will look negatively upon an entrepreneur who enlists the help of others in performing such tasks.

Among the more attractive benefits of the modern "new economy" style incubators, aside from the availability of seed capital, is the option to become part of a keiretsu. A keiretsu is a network of businesses that own stakes in each other's companies and do business together. This type of affiliation can be a great way to jump-start your market penetration. It can lead to faster revenue, earlier customers, and a stronger profit and loss statement during your money-raising efforts. However, a keiretsu does have the drawback of creating a potential chasm between making sales to your old network and making sales to mainstream market customers.

Although most incubators have similar services to offer, not all incubators are created alike. Many have only some of the services we have discussed and those that have all of the services can be very costly in equity. Incubators fall into both the nonprofit and for-profit categories. Oftentimes, the nonprofit incubators are real estate plays or university campus incubators that offer a range of services including office space at a low cost. These incubators usually do not provide capital or a keiretsu. They are inexpensive and may be useful to you if the location or particular services they offer are convenient.

The for-profit incubators fall into two categories: open incubators and private incubators. An open incubator is one that outside ventures can seek to join or utilize in order to raise capital. Examples of open incubators include CMGI (at least formerly when they called themselves an incubator) and Flip Filipowski's Divine Interventures. A private for-profit incubator, on the other hand, is one that creates its own ventures and maintains a controlling share in most of its holdings. Outside ventures normally do not seek capital from these incubators. Examples of such incubators include IdeaLab, creator of eToys, NetZero, a host of companies that live off of Internet advertising, and Incube8.com of Baltimore, MD, a small private incubator focused on the e-commerce area. There are some for-profit companies that assist start-ups and are, in fact, not incubators at all. For example, despite the popular notion that it is an incubator, Garage.com (now known as Garage Technology Ventures) is a venture capital investment bank that helps place investors with companies who need capital.

Business incubators are a popular option for many early stage companies, but not for everyone. When should a venture make use of an incubator? You could most likely benefit from the services of an incubator if one or more of the following applies:

- you are scientist with technology, but you lack a team;
- you have technology but would like someone else to take it forward; or
- you need to bootstrap (save money).

If you have a more developed or in-depth venture, perhaps you can still benefit from an incubator. In this case, you will need to carefully weigh the pros and cons of enlisting one.

Powerize.com started out in a university incubator—the University of Maryland Technology Advancement Program. The company made use of a program University of Maryland called the "business plan review." We remained with this program for one year and paid a total of $6,000 for rent and Internet access. One percent of the company's equity went to the university. The biggest benefit we received was access to the university's computer science students. In the end, we hired several—their salaries were relatively inexpensive and they were very productive. We also collaborated with a faculty member on product testing. Another advantage to using this incubator was that the location. It was very central to the employees and resources we needed. After one year the company was growing far too rapidly and we opted to move. Overall, however, it was an excellent experience.

Another alternative, perhaps a favorable one for the majority of entrepreneurs with new ventures, is to create your own incubator. As I previously mentioned, ConQuest started out in a mattress factory. Our rent was less than our phone bill. We received limited funds from the state of Maryland, but the greatest result of the experience was the realization that we were resourceful enough to make a little go a long way. This knowledge served us well as we faced future obstacles.

Most good incubators will have a focus or area of expertise. The better ones have, at the very least, a network, if not a keiretsu. And the most sought-after incubators have their own investment funds and a real keiretsu. This kind of incubator is extremely valuable to almost any venture, provided that the incubator has the right focus area—that is, one that matches the company's vision.

What is a keiretsu?

The word *keiretsu* is a Japanese term originally given as a label for a powerful network of closely related companies that support each other strategically. They are often created by a bank or venture capital fund. Members of the keiretsu are independent but work together to penetrate markets and fend off competition. The members of this organization often do business with each other, offering discounts and special deals.

Unlike the Japanese keiretsu, the Western or "new economy" keiretsu is more loosely coupled with no company or banker in complete control of the network. Oftentimes, the executives of these companies share information and experiences freely within the keiretsu, acting as a sort of business clique. These networks enjoy business advantages such as accelerated sales from other keiretsu companies as customers, stronger forces against competition, and assistance from the network in forming powerful alliances. The best way for a new venture to become a part of a keiretsu is for it to be funded by the venture capital group that spawns the keiretsu. Kliener Perkins Caufield & Byers is especially known for using the keiretsu concept to develop its ventures. In fact, this company was a powerful force in creating the Internet bubble using a keiretsu effect with its investments in Netscape, Amazon.com, Excite, Sun, and other key Internet bellwethers. CMGI is also known for operating a keiretsu of companies in the new economy and supporting these companies with its advertising resources.

Leveraging Your Network

We have been talking about high-flying ways to get leverage—equity, motivation, advisors, incubators. However, don't overlook the power of your own personal network! The old saying about getting business in your own backyard applies. Early stage ventures need a significant effort to gain traction and become established. Leveraging your network can be one of the best ways to achieve early traction. In fact, your network can be considered an extension of your team. To gain critical mass and the work intensity necessary to drive your venture forward, you need to harness your entire virtual team.

A lot of latent power lies within your network, and your network is probably more extensive than you think. It includes employees, customers, consultants, club members, former professors, colleagues, neighbors, accountants, lawyers, service professionals, local universities, etc. Remember the "law of seven" (i.e. someone you know knows someone who knows someone who knows … the president.) One contact could put you in touch with anyone. Using your network to recruit staff, customers, investors, alliances, exposure opportunities, advisors, and suppliers, you can create your extended team.

Attending networking events, conferences, professional happy hours, workshops, and breakfast meetings is another highly effective way to extend your network. I mentioned earlier that Powerize.com hired the Adrenaline Group to help with meeting a development goal. I met Scott McLoughlin—or "McScott," as I refer to him—at the Baltimore Washington Venture Group Networking Breakfast about a week before our company needed him. My attendance to that event paid off because we found the immediate help we needed.

As I got to know McScott, I learned that he frequently attended professional events like those I listed above. His presence at these events, combined with his outgoing personality, led to the astounding marketing success of the Adrenaline Group, which otherwise was consisted mostly of engineers. McScott, too, was an engineer, and one who contributed actively in development. But he was also the CEO of the Adrenaline Group and he did all of the company's marketing. He is one of those rare birds that can do both marketing and engineering.

Your team is not just *your* team. It consists of you, your vision, your employees, and your advisors. People who should not be forgotten are your investors, service providers, your keiretsu, and your extended team. Small ventures can accomplish a lot when they leverage an extended network. This virtual team will provide you with greater strength. Use it to your advantage!

Chapter 3

Leveraging the Horizon

"Never look down to test the ground before taking your next step; only he who keeps his eye fixed on the far horizon will find the right road."
—Dag Hammarskjold

"Leveraging the horizon" refers to the act of using the far horizon to guide the implementation of a vision while simultaneously using today's marketplace as a reference point. Stretching to the horizon while taking one solid step at a time is a great method to use when developing your venture. Doing so will enable you to move into progressive and uncharted territory with a vision that is innovative, yet achievable in today's market. This chapter provides a framework for creative thought and positioning in regards to the concept of leveraging the horizon.

Innovation: Leveraging the Horizon

Let us consider two technology ventures from the mid-90s, each with a different product strategy. We'll use fictitious names for the purposes of this discussion and call the first venture Data Semantics, Inc. and the second Transaction Imaging Corporation.

Data Semantics was the developer and provider of a new database management tool called a semantic data model. Its product was intended to replace or complement relational and object-oriented databases with a new technology. The other venture, Transaction Imaging, developed a document imaging system specialized for banks and financial institutions. Both ventures suffered from product positioning difficulties but their difficulties were of opposing natures.

Industry pundits often call complicated technology "bleeding-edge technology" because the technology has no market and therefore bleeds cash. Data Semantics was a bleeding-edge venture. The company's technology was so far out on the horizon that there was a huge gap between its vision and the relational database technology that the mainstream market used at the time. Oracle, IBM, Microsoft, Sybase, and Informix are all examples of major established companies that pioneered relational database technology. However, that type of technology was not the only option available. A new class of database technology called "object-oriented databases" was on the horizon that uses views of related data called "objects." Object-oriented databases had difficulty succeeding because the technology was further out on the horizon than mainstream database technology.

Data Semantics had a type of technology—semantic data models—that was even *further* out on the horizon. It was attempting to sell a technology that was more intricate, convoluted, and advanced than object-oriented databases, which was also having a difficult time displacing relational database technology. Not only did Data Semantics have a far-out horizon, it also soared to the edge of the horizon right away. That was its greatest mistake. Several major corporations wanted to adopt their technology but didn't because it was too risky. They did not want to be the sole users of this technology and be locked into a company with so few customers. The risk of bankruptcy was too great. In the end Data Semantics failed because its horizon was too far ahead of the mainstream buyers.

Transaction Imaging, on the other hand, was a "me-too" venture. Its product was one of hundreds of document imaging systems on the market. The company's only product differentiation was based upon the latest new feature they had added to their software—the same feature that several thousand other small software companies had added to their software.

Transaction Imaging had a sharp demonstration and they landed their first few clients based upon personal relationships. Eventually, most of the components they built for document imaging systems became freely available in programming environments offered by Microsoft and other vendors. Transaction Imaging failed because its horizon was too shortsighted. In fact, the entire document imaging market collapsed, with the demise of Wang as a prime example. There was little differentiation between offerings and the software eventually became commoditized. Anyone could buy a scanner for $99 and a multi-Gigabyte hard drive for a few hundred bucks. Voila! You have a document imaging system that in yesterday's market collected hundreds of thousands of dollars in product and service fees.

The concept of "leveraging the horizon" points to an area somewhere between these two extremes: the bleeding-edge venture and the me-too venture. The me-too venture lacks a horizon that transcends today's established marketplace. The bleeding-edge venture has a horizon that exceeds the needs of the marketplace.

What type of venture will succeed? Refer to the quote at the beginning of the chapter. It instructs you to keep your eyes fixed on the horizon before taking your next step. It also tells you not to look down. That's what the me-too venture does. The quote implies that you shouldn't just go straight to the horizon either. That's what the bleeding-edge venture does. Instead, you must take steps methodically. The best approach is to slowly advance from today's marketplace while being guided by the horizon.

The horizon is your vision for a new business derived from the advantage of your new technology. This approach is designed to create a discontinuous advance in technology and/or a business concept that is positioned to be a manageable although significant leap forward from the current playing field.

In *Innovation*, Richard Foster describes the science of—you guessed it—innovation. He differentiates between an evolution and a revolution. Evolution, he surmises, is an incremental advance while a revolution is a radical and fundamental change. I advocate creating a revolutionary vision that stretches from an evolutionary starting point.

Foster illustrates how this can be achieved with the famous S-curve for technology, whereby a technological venture undergoes a long period of incubation, a rapid growth, and then a maturation or saturation at the end of its cycle. A disruption occurs when a new technology, having an S-curve that lies above and beyond the present technology, enters into the market. The diagram below illustrates the concept of innovation as the leap from one S-curve to the next, as distinct from optimization, which is merely advancement along the present S-curve.

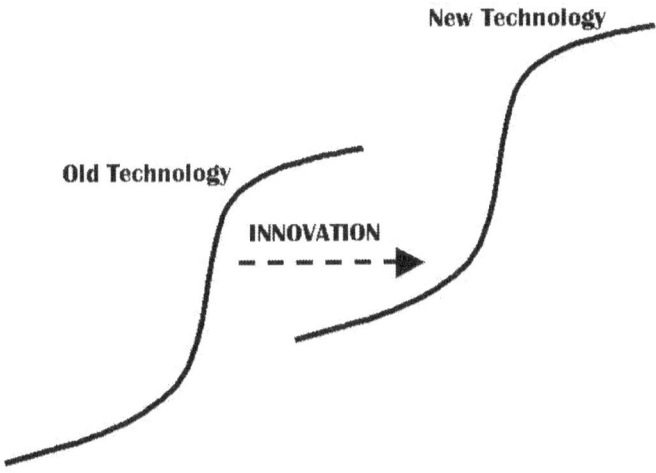

After establishing your horizon and deciding what barriers you are going to face take a look at your venture plan and try to determine where the discontinuity in the S-curve lies. Is it a significant but manageable step to cross the chasm between early adopters and mainstream acceptance? Is it a leap in technology, business model, or both? What are you going to sell? To whom? Why are they going to buy it?

Gary Hamel in *Leading the Revolution* defines a revolution as a change in which "business concept innovation" takes place. Such business concept innovation may or may not be driven by a discontinuous technology. The abstract principles of S-curves may be thought to apply to business models as well as technology. You must proceed with caution or your plight may be the same as that of Data Semantics. New paradigms, as they are sometimes referred, have a high failure rate. Just ask about 90 percent of the founders of dot-com ventures, many of whom became disillusioned by market mania and started to believe that a mere sleight of hand causes an automatic business tidal wave. Perhaps most illustrative of this mania was the spectacular rise and fall of IdeaLab's eToys, a company that seemingly arose from nowhere, but later became hailed as the first mover for toys on the Web. After a temporary Wall Street delusion that eToys was worth more than traditional rivals like Toys 'R Us, it had an equally spectacular fall from grace, as did many of the dot-coms that purported to be taking over an industry simply because they sold on the Internet before the traditional players.

We are talking about a discontinuous advance in technology and/or business concept, but an advance positioned such that the discontinuity is a manageable although significant step from the current playing field.

In order to succeed using a new approach, discontinuous technology, or business concept innovation, one needs to venture into uncharted territory with a venture that replaces an old way, meets a new need, or changes a business model. Which barriers are you going to surmount? Create a venture that is a discontinuous innovation, one that provides a product of value that people today are willing to use. While looking for discontinuous technology and/or a business model, also look for continuity with the marketplace today. A smooth transition with an obvious launch point from the mainstream marketplace to your technology is ideal.

ConQuest Software advanced the accuracy of search engines using artificial intelligence. While the software was feature-rich, it could be used like any other search engine in its default-operating mode. It had an advanced search mode that required a little more work on the part of the user but in return it provided dramatically improved results. ConQuest's discontinuous innovation was the use of electronic dictionaries to build a semantic network that improved the accuracy of search results. This network linked the meaning of words together and searched for concepts *related* to the defined search terms. This software product was successfully sold to government intelligence agencies, online publishers, and research institutions, as well as a variety of applications such as litigation support.

When ConQuest was founded, our vision was to build a software system with the ability to understand written text and use it to perform various tasks. The first application for this product was information retrieval. At the time, the most popular method of information retrieval was known as Boolean keyword search—the retrieval of information using certain keywords without regard to their meaning or context. Still widely used on the Web, this method of searching is known by information retrieval scientists to recall about 25 percent of the available information for a tolerable search result list. The "horizon" of ConQuest's vision was to enable users to ask a question and receive matches that did not merely locate the word, but answered the question as well. Early Internet company Ask Jeeves illustrates that this task essentially cannot be done with today's technology and knowledge bases.

To leverage the horizon, ConQuest chose to seek more accurate search results using natural language queries. It was first appreciated by power users, but use of the product readily spread throughout the intelligence community, the publishing world, and eventually the corporate world after ConQuest's merger with Excalibur. This technology is now offered by Convera (Nasdaq: CNVR), a joint venture between Excalibur and Intel to provide total solutions to digital asset management.

Can you imagine a future in which your vision is fully realized? And then, can you imagine taking the first significant step toward that vision without becoming overly preoccupied about today's rat race? Can you implement this step in a way that is continuous with your customers' needs today? Answering these questions is a good way to begin visualizing your horizon and then leveraging it to define where you should begin. Before continuing, reread the quote at the beginning of this chapter to reinforce the importance of staying focused on the horizon.

Knowing Where Your Market Is Today

If you followed the recommendation in the previous sentence you were reminded that you should never look at the ground when taking the next step. You must let your horizon, not the ground, guide you. Another reason you need not look down is that you should already know the ground very well. You should be familiar with your market, the technology in your marketplace, the players and competition, their business models, their pricing systems, and the products that customers are buying. It is very difficult to leverage your horizon if you don't know your starting point.

You must figure out where your market is headed and then get in front of it.

There are plenty of ways to obtain knowledge about your starting point but the quality of the information you seek must be sound. It must be researched extensively and objectively. Ultimately, it will contribute to your knowledge and confidence, as discussed in the first chapter of this book. Methods of expanding your knowledge concerning the market and current technology include:

- working in the industry for several years,
- attending industry trade shows,
- researching the industry on the Web,
- reading the market reports in the industry,
- talking to the customers or users,
- using the current products yourself, and
- reading annual reports of public companies.

This task of gaining market insight is very important. You cannot deliver a better product or service if you don't know the needs of the market. You cannot expand the market with a new business concept if you don't know the boundaries. You cannot even visualize your horizon in the proper context without this information and experience. You must figure out where your market is headed and then get in front of it. Of course, be careful not to make the mistake of a bleeding-edge venture whose technology exceeds market needs. Don't go so far ahead that the cost of trailblazing and market discontinuity completely undermine your probability of success.

One of the best ways to establish a benchmark is to attend trade shows. You can listen to the industry pundits speak, walk the show floor and see what vendors are pushing. You can talk to people and ask questions. You can try products yourself and buy publications and studies that are available. To maximize the benefits of such events, attend several different shows. There are academic conferences that discuss technology and science and market shows that promote products and reach end users. You can also find some niche shows on specialized areas within your field.

The following chart lists some fundamental questions that you should be able to answer as you begin your venture. This chart is intended to give you probing questions as you research your market. There are numerous books and resources on market research and business planning that you can refer to for a more in-depth treatment of this subject. Try *The*

Successful Business Plan, by Rhonda Abrahms, or *Launching New Ventures,* by Kathleen Allen.

Fundamental Questions to Answer Before Launching a Venture

- What are the trends in your industry?
- What strategic opportunities exist in your industry today?
- How large is your industry and what is its growth rate?
- Who are your competitors and what do they offer?
- Do you know the limits of your competitors' approaches?
- How sensitive is your industry to economic cycles? Seasonality?
- What are the regulatory barriers in your industry?
- What is the nature of the supply and distribution channels in the industry?
- What is the demographic and geographic distribution of your market?
- What are the purchasing patterns of your potential customers?
- How large is your market segment?
- How is market share distributed among your potential competitors?
- Are there any barriers to entry that exist in your market?

Establishing Your Horizon

Most likely now more than ever the spirit of innovation is soaring within you. At this point you might have a high-level business vision, perhaps some proprietary technology and a semblance of a business concept revolution to drive it. All of these necessary components come from your vision, your passion, listening to potential customers, astutely observing a market need, or perhaps they come from your own experiences and frustrations with the market. You have identified a market pain that your venture will relieve. Now you are ready to paint the picture of your horizon, write your manifesto, and prepare yourself for some zealous—and hopefully exhilarating—selling.

> **As the founder, you have to be the best salesman in your company. However, you may not always be selling your product. You may be selling your vision with the hope of reaching your horizon.**

If you are one of those technocrats who shudders at the notion of having to do sales, it's high time to change your attitude. Selling is not only for the crackerjack salesman who is unable to do anything else or the telemarketer that calls you at dinnertime. In this book, I am not referring to that kind of selling. I'm talking about the type of sales that will be the lifeblood of your enterprise. If that makes you want to bolt back to the bosom of your corporate employer, then perhaps you need to assess what "selling" means to you.

As the founder, you have to be the best salesman in the company. However, you may not always be selling your product. You may be selling your vision with the hope of reaching your horizon. In doing so, it is crucial that your enthusiasm and your passion shine through. The horizon must become a place of Nirvana for those who buy into your vision. You'll need to sell your idea to attract management, employees, customers, suppliers, beta testers, investors, as well as to secure loans and gain access to public markets. This type of selling originates from your vision and your horizon. Therefore, it is imperative that you clarify your vision and horizon right from the start.

Defining the Horizon

So you have a vision. You know your technology. You know where your market is today. Maybe you have part of your founding team. You're getting revved up and ready to go. But wait! Have you really defined your horizon? Some people refer to the horizon as your vision statement. Your vision statement is distinct from your mission statement in that it does not merely consist of the operating goals you set, but of the big picture and the ultimate goal.

In order to devise the definition of your horizon—your vision statement—there are two prime considerations that should be addressed. These are:

1. What is your technical/product innovation, or what is the S-curve discontinuity that you are harnessing? Where will this venture ultimately lead you given unlimited time and success?
2. What is the business process revolution or business model that you will use to implement your vision in such a way that you sidestep your competition? How could this procedure potentially transform the market given unlimited time and money?

By thinking in this manner, you will enable yourself to formulate a compelling vision statement. This statement will be your horizon, the place upon which you keep your eyes fixed as you conduct your business.

Consider D-Fusion, a small start-up near Baltimore. It spun out of Johns Hopkins University in 2000 with a distributed processing technology developed on Defense Advanced Research Projects Agency (DARPA) funding. D-Fusion recognized a problem with information on the Internet. It gets stale. Most large search engines take thirty to sixty days to fully crawl the Web and even then they miss much of the dynamic content. D-Fusion's vision is to make an engine able to crawl the entire Web, including the dynamic content, in less than twenty-four hours. Their discontinuous technology innovation suggests using meta computing—that is, harnessing the idle power of *millions* of computers to distribute the workload. Their business concept innovation is to rent this service to search engines, Web sites, and corporate customers. Why is this venture a business model disruption in the industry? Simply because it undercuts everyone who performs this service themselves, everyone who gets inferior performance for a greater cost, and also everyone who doesn't do it at all. This business shares the cost across many customers, therefore making it a compelling value proposition.

Technological innovation can be assessed by tracking the funding and research projects of the National Science Foundation (NSF), DARPA, National Aeronautics and Space Association (NASA), National Institute of Health (NIH), and any other government agencies that fund technology development and scientific research. By following the research of these organizations, you can test your knowledge of the current technology as well as compare the research to the emerging discontinuous breakthroughs in the field. Following this research can also be a source of stimulating ideas, since oftentimes the researchers funded by these agencies are not entrepreneurs, and they never will be. Many successful companies were started through funding from some of these agencies. For example, SUN Microsystems was heavily funded by DARPA in its early days.

Business concept innovation is not so easily catalogued. Through your market research, you may find information on business models that are currently in use. As far as new models are concerned, they must come from your imagination, based upon your understanding of the market. Perhaps you can co-opt ideas from other fields, but ultimately your vision needs its own unique definition. Gary Hamel in *Leading the Revolution* explores various ways of creating new business concepts—for instance, by writing a manifesto. He states that innovation should be pictured in terms of novel business concepts and competition should be pictured as a contest between business models.

ConQuest's merger with Excalibur occurred during a very competitive and pivotal time in Internet history, and each company's business concept innovation influenced its outcome. Our key competitors at the time were Verity, a Mountainview, CA company that sold a product for "concept based searching" of corporate information; and Fulcrum Technologies, a Canadian company that achieved its early success through distribution relationships. A new competitor called Architext emerged out of Stanford, CA with Kleiner Perkins funding. Architext could retrieve novel information based upon statistical processing. However, it found itself up against immediate entrenched competition from ConQuest, Verity, and Fulcrum, among other companies.

In order to establish your horizon, you may look to technology innovation or business concept innovation, but the most powerful horizons are comprised of both.

Kleiner Perkins worked with Architext to redefine its business model entirely. As a result they decided to index the entire Internet and rename their company Excite. Excite, as an early mover in the Internet search engine market, went on to become a multi-billion-dollar valued Internet company. Excalibur management opted not to index the Internet at the same time as Excite. While both Verity and Excalibur succeeded in their own business models, their success was not as spectacular as that of Excite. And despite the fact that Architext and ConQuest both had roots in search engine technology, in the end the two companies were not even in the same market. Business concept innovation can make an enormous difference in your venture's ultimate market, its valuation, and its success or failure.

In order to establish your horizon, you may look to technology innovation or business concept innovation, but the most powerful horizons are comprised of both. The development of your horizon may require a discontinuous technology or a novel business concept. Most likely it will be derived from your experience and knowledge, combined with thinking radically or perhaps just instinctively knowing the needs of today's market.

Sometimes your horizon can be derived from the observation of a problem or the realization that something is ridiculously difficult and can be simplified. Jim Clark established Healtheon (now part of WebMD) partially due to his frustrations with the healthcare system. Why couldn't the Internet be used to file claims, connect physicians directly to payers, link pharmacies to physicians' offices, schedule appointments for laboratory tests, and provide laboratory results—all in one integrated system? That was the business plan of Healtheon, which raised money almost solely on Jim Clark's reputation. However, taking on the $2 trillion healthcare industry in one fell swoop proved to be more than one company could handle, especially given investors' expectations about the speed of the Internet. The merger between WebMD and Healtheon has formed a company with similar ambitions. Although the company has had its ups and downs, positive progress is being made and WebMD/Healtheon continues to stretch toward its horizon.

Not all companies need be established on such a grand scale or mammoth horizon. Enter a small, five-person former company near Washington, D.C. called Sensory Scapes. The founder of Sensory Scapes had a vision derived from his personal experiences: he wanted to bring the effects of nature into healing environments. It has been established by research that the sight and sound of nature accelerates recovery from diseases and provides some degree of pain relief. With its horizon in mind, Sensory Scapes created a natural image display designed primarily for healthcare facilities, waiting rooms, spas, and healing rooms. Sensory Scapes recreates the sights, sounds, and scents of nature. The scapes feature stunning photography that is displayed in a lighted enclosure and enhanced with multimedia effects. One of Sensory Scape's main sales propositions is that a hospital need not undergo a multimillion-dollar physical renovation to add nature to its setting, therefore depicting its product as a practical, inexpensive alternative.

It can be highly instructive to analyze other companies to see how they are leveraging their horizons. Think of some small, high-tech ventures with which you are personally familiar. For each venture, think about what makes it promising. What is its horizon? Where is it operating today? What discontinuous technology does it present? What business concept innovation is it deploying? Do you think it will be a success in the future? Why or why not?

Stretching into New Territory

I have advocated establishing a vision of the horizon. And I have cautioned you not to jump too far out right away but instead use your horizon as a guide as you proceed. Now I am going to add just a little more philosophy to this concept.

Once you have taken a step and established yourself on firm ground, you will need to keep pushing towards the horizon. But you need only to stretch, not make a colossal leap. Implement what works—and stretch it 10 percent. And when that starts working, stretch it again.

This technique will keep you on the leading edge and away from the bleeding edge. You will be leapfrogging your competition, but at the same time, remaining on solid ground. Keep the rest simple. Remember that the excitement and vision of your breakthrough will power the team and your stakeholders. Your business is powered by the ability of mainstream markets to accept it. Read the box about Celera Genomics for an example in which stretching to stay ahead doubled as a stretch to a simpler technological method.

Celera Genomics

By the late nineties, the government-sponsored Human Genome Project was having early success. However the government, not the private sector, organized it. As a result it was a widely distributed network of academics who had objectives other than finishing the project and advancing the field of medicine and healthcare. The National Institute of Health had projected a completion date somewhere near 2005.

Enter Craig Venter, a brilliant maverick geneticist who got his start on the public Human Genome Project. Recognizing that 2005 was a long way away and that millions of lives could be saved or improved with an earlier completion date, Dr. Venter advocated shot-gunning, a new technique for sequencing the genome. Using Dr. Venter's technique, the speed of sequencing the genome could be vastly improved at the expense of a slightly lower fidelity of data. The ivory tower moral philosophers of the public project fought against Dr. Venter's technique because it was scientifically less advanced and had the risk of improperly sequencing the genome near regions of high repeat sequences.

Fortunately, Dr. Venter decided to break free of the government research and received venture capital funding to start Celera Genomics. This new outgrowth led to a race between Celera Genomics, a company that was developing a commercial venture, and the Human Genome Project. Pride and scientific competitiveness drove the project's contributors. The result? The human genome was sequenced by early 2001, several years ahead of schedule. Dr. Venter's tactics shaved years off the genome project, not only saving tax dollars, but also accelerating medical advances and potentially saving millions of lives—while creating a multibillion-dollar company.

In the end, the joint efforts of Celera and the Human Genome Project contributed to the completion of the task. But the credit for the sooner-than-expected medical advances, tax dollar savings, and acceleration of the commercial genomics industry goes to Dr. Venter. Despite the competitive nature of the race, this accomplishment illustrates the kind of government-to-commercial tradeoff that can result from government funding initiatives. Many, if not most, government programs do not end with such spectacular commercial industry launches. The approach of Celera Genomics is a prime example of an S-curve discontinuity and stretching to leverage the horizon.

Establishing Proprietary Value

Dot-coms strayed a little from believing that they needed anything proprietary. Venture capitalists funded many me-too ventures and insisted only on some novel business model that might work. The lesson has been learned. Today it is expected that you have a proprietary position that sets you apart from competition, not only to attract major funding, but also to provide a competitive advantage for your company. The proprietary value of a company is usually based on technology or intellectual property, but in some cases it can also be based on business concept innovation.

> **The lesson has been learned. Today it is expected that you have a proprietary position that sets you apart from competition.**

When innovation is defined around S-curve discontinuities, the discontinuity defines the proprietary value. To achieve business success with discontinuous innovation, it needs to be translated to an improvement in the widely accepted concept of customer value chain or business processes leading to the ultimate product.

In *Competitive Advantage*, Michael Porter defines the value chain as a high-level model of how businesses receive raw materials through various processes and assemble and sell products to customers. The customer value chain includes all aspects of the product's transit along this path, including logistics, operations, marketing and sales, and customer service. A critical prerequisite for success in the digital economy is the implementation of an *integrated value chain* that extends across—and beyond—the enterprise. For example, Microsoft broke the S-curve on operating systems several times—first with DOS and then with Windows. Its proprietary position on the market surrounds the operating system, but its superior marketing—based on high volume and low price—has been responsible for its unmatched success.

When innovation is defined around a business process revolution, the proprietary value is directly implanted by an improvement in the value chain delivered to the customer. This sort of proprietary value may be harder to defend because it is difficult to obtain a patent to prevent competition from doing the same thing. For example, Dell has attained its remarkable success in the PC industry by mastering the process of selling PCs over the Web and providing its customers with the exact configuration they want. Dell improved the customer value chain by reducing the cost of marketing and providing superior customer service.

Most early stage high-tech ventures attain their proprietary position through S-curve discontinuity. This position is far easier to achieve when new, innovative, and patent-worthy technology is involved. Often, proof-of-principle demonstrations and successive prototyping are helpful in achieving a proprietary position. Of course, it must all start with a well-thought-out idea based on thorough knowledge of the technical discipline involved. In fact, most high-tech ventures begin with a talented engineer who has a bright idea, which is fine as long as the team is properly balanced later. The most ideal technical proprietary position is one that competition cannot mimic without great risk and expense, or one that is solidly protected by a patent position.

The government has established a number of programs to provide funding for the early development of high-risk technology. These programs are often the best sources of early development dollars for the seed-stage venture that does not yet have a product ready for the market. Perhaps the best known of these sources is the Small Business Innovation Research (SBIR) program. The SBIR program consists of a proof-of-concept phase, followed by a second development phase. Each phase has to be earned through the submission of a successful proposal, and ultimately, 10 percent of these proposals are funded.

ConQuest developed its entire product set through a series of approximately eight SBIR awards before going for venture capital funding. The intent of the SBIR program is to provide funding for technologies that will later be commercialized. ConQuest was an SBIR success in that respect. Unfortunately, much of the SBIR funding is awarded to research and development firms that never successfully commercialize their products.

These funding sources are best used when they are applied to companies with a commercial intent from the outset, and those that use the funding to do applied research in order to further develop their technology. It is important not to use these funding sources for basic research, but for applied research later on, where the goal is to prepare a technology that has already been through basic research for commercialization. Specific sources of funding will be discussed in the chapter on financing.

It is vital that your proprietary technology or S-curve discontinuity advantage is spelled out in layman's terms. Oftentimes an engineer will understand the significance of the technology, but will only be able to speak in technocratic terms. A clear description is vital for communicating your vision, marketing your product, filing for a patent, and conveying a sense of success and power about your company. As your technology is developed, the benefits and features should be clearly articulated.

You should make a concentrated effort to protect your proprietary value. This book cannot substitute a quality resource on intellectual property protection by any means. But a few high-level suggestions are in order.

You should always file for patent protection whenever you can. Having a patent-pending status can help with your marketing message and, eventually, being awarded a patent may help with raising funds. The most important reason to file for patent protection is for defensive purposes. You do not want someone else to turn up with a patent on your business concept or technology.

Incidentally, it became popular to apply for business concept patents when Priceline.com filed for a patent on the reverse auction-pricing concept on the Web. These patents are exceedingly difficult to obtain due to their typically broad, sweeping claims. If you are contemplating a patent position on a business process innovation, consult your patent attorney for advice.

Other areas of intellectual property protection that should be pursued are copyright protection, trademarking, and trade secrets protection. Many companies will rely on nondisclosure agreements to protect trade secrets. This practice is a very common one in the high-tech world, used primarily as a good faith gesture. It is rare that a real case is ever brought about due to nondisclosure agreements (NDA). As a matter of principle, I have made a policy of not signing NDAs over the years and using personal relationships, rather than legal threats, as a means of business discussion. However, this tactic does not work for all personality types.

Staying Focused

With your eyes on your horizon and your proprietary position established, it is finally time to push forward. One of the most common problems of small companies is the inability to stay focused. Cash flow pressures, new ideas, and unexpected opportunities cause them to wander astray. However, a small company with limited resources cannot afford to do too many things. As history attests, companies that are able to achieve laser-sharp focus are those that can drive the furthest. Therefore you should put all the wood behind the arrow. Focus all available resources in the company on the same thing. This includes company operational schedules, engineering projects, trade shows, management communications, and yes, even senior sales professionals. By focusing everyone on the idea of achieving a similar objective, you will be able to observe the productivity that results.

In *The Northbound Train*, Karl Albrecht provides an excellent methodology for building team consensus on where the company is headed—and putting everyone on the *same* "northbound train." The importance of a common focus cannot be overemphasized.

To achieve focus, everyone in the company must concentrate on the task at hand. I am not referring to financial focus or bottom-line focus, but rather keeping your eyes on the horizon and following it. Maintaining focus is analogous to a team of people rowing a boat. If one person on the team attempts to row in a different direction than the others, the entire direction of the boat changes.

Putting all the wood behind the arrow means focusing all available resources in the company on the same thing.

Some lessons from ConQuest are useful to illustrate this concept. In ConQuest's early days, our eager VP Sales sold our unreleased product as a document manager, in a distributed database environment, and for a CD-ROM application. The problem was that ConQuest was a search engine that ran on a UNIX server. Our product did not meet the requirements for any of those three applications. However, because we were cash-strapped and we needed the money, we proceeded to focus the engineering team on delivering the applications specified by our VP Sales. This change of plans caused us to establish a second engineering group whose mission was to tailor the product to the customer and build user interfaces. Not only did this splinter our group into many different directions, it did not work. ConQuest finally got back on track when we agreed to stick to a few applications that we could perform well. But this agreement did not come about without causing a rift. We lost three or four good people over it.

Powerize.com had some similar challenges. The company was founded to build an information server for corporations. When the first product was delayed several times in engineering development, the company decided to make an acquisition in order to accelerate its business. Powerize.com bought two content services from IBM's Internet Services Group—IBM infoMarket™ and Lotus Newsstand™. Our underlying intent was to accelerate our company's initial product, but the result was that the company had three products and only fifty employees. Eventually, in order to consolidate our efforts, we merged these products into a single Internet portal called Powerize.com, which is now part of Hoovers, Inc. Once Powerize.com established its business Internet portal, an additional focus problem began to haunt us.

We had a business development staff who was responsible for third-party distribution. Our product offering was a snap on, or a set of tools that enabled other Web sites to access our content. But our business development staff had a habit of offering new features with each sale, despite the fact that we didn't yet have these features available. The result was that we were constantly developing to suit the customer's needs, rather than to provide a stable product.

How do you strike a balance between being innovative and staying focused? Keep in mind your real motivation, allow incremental innovation, but at the same time be very decisive about high-risk innovation and change of course. You need to be successful with your first endeavor before risking the company on another. After narrowing down your ideas, execution becomes more important than brainstorming new ideas. Now is the time when you need to avoid the temptation to implement a series of new ideas and radical changes. This advice does not mean that you shouldn't respond to new developments in the marketplace. Sometimes, the market demands that you shift your plans. It must be done carefully, however. An especially illustrative example of the need for caution when changing your plans is Netscape's constant positional shifting in response to Microsoft's competitive attacks.

Netscape was a browser company. When Microsoft offered Internet Explorer for free, Netscape was forced to do the same, and therefore needed a source of revenue. To obtain this revenue, the company stepped up sales in corporate server products and then started an Internet portal. This move put them in three distinct businesses: Internet browsers, Internet portals, and corporate Web servers. It's very difficult for a young company to be good at all three. Microsoft's bullying eventually forced Netscape to sell out to AOL for a paltry $4 billion. What a shame!

Put all the wood behind the arrow. Achieving sharp focus is absolutely essential to the success of a small start-up venture. Continuously maintain your focus on your horizon and all else should fall into place.

Chapter 4

Writing in the Sand

"When we walk to the edge of all the light we have and take that step into the darkness of the unknown, we must believe that one of two things will happen: There will be something solid for us to stand on, or we will learn how to fly."
—Laura Thompson Foy

The business plan is an essential tool. It encapsulates and articulates your horizon, vision, and operational plan. A business plan should not be the company Bible, however. It is relevant only to the present point in time. You should view your business plan as more of a compass than a road map. It points you in the right direction and, at the same time, communicates your vision and validates your business model. The business plan should not be a road map because as you travel down the road the landscape will change. You will constantly face the decision of whether to modify your direction or stick to your plan. Such decisions are not easy ones to make.

At the 1992 annual meeting of the Information Industry Association in San Francisco, Don MacLagan—then current chairman and CEO of NewsEdge Corporation—gave a speech on business planning. In his talk he said that business planning is like writing in the sand. Such a concept exemplifies the theory that a business plan is an ongoing process, not an end product. This chapter addresses the importance of the business plan and how its development truly is an ongoing process. Later in this chapter, you will be exposed to some ideas on how to maintain a business plan that changes frequently. You will also be introduced to some of the tools needed in order to perform this task efficiently.

Before undertaking the important task of writing a business plan, read Rhonda Abrams's book *The Successful Business Plan*. Abrams provides a structured explanation about each component of a business plan, as well as ninety-nine detailed forms to be filled out by the reader that will force him or her to organize the necessary information for developing a business plan.

Iterative Business Planning and Chaos

One of the few times to use your business plan as a static document is as a reference point for when you decide to raise capital. At all other times it must be viewed as a living document that is constantly maintained, updated, and communicated to the entire company staff. Think of it as a working document with many authors.

In order to be useful, a business plan must respond to the changing conditions in the market, the capital position of the company, state of product development, and more. It is vitally important that this *process* be mastered because it is a key part of management. That doesn't mean you should constantly change the vision of your company. It just means that you need to navigate the market and product realities as you go.

When embarking on the development of your business plan, you should continually focus on the same horizon as when you began the venture. Your vantage point may have shifted, but you should still be viewing the same horizon. Perhaps your proprietary advantage turned out to be in a different area than originally thought. Maybe the customer adoption rate is slower or faster than you expected. Your company is part of a dynamic and unpredictable marketplace. Your business plan must be flexible enough to adapt to these constantly changing conditions.

Never, ever, ever use a specialized writing software package to develop your business plan.

Before going any further, I want to drive home one very important concept: Never, ever, ever use a specialized writing software package to develop your business plan. Unless you are manufacturing toilet paper and the business plan is the toilet paper itself, do not even open one of these packages. Write the business plan yourself! Do not hire this task out. The business plan is based upon *your* vision; therefore, it must be written and maintained by the principal operating management of the company, i.e. you. One exception: a software package can—and should—be used to generate financial projections, provided that you develop the assumptions underlying the model.

Although the business plan will continually change, your first business plan is an important milestone. It expresses your horizon as a business vision and it provides the framework for implementing your mission. Many ventures find that either the company vision changes, an unexpected alteration in the marketplace occurs, a new product has unanticipated value, or, in the case of the Internet, the market simply evolves quickly. All of these factors can easily render a well-done business plan obsolete in just a few months. When that happens, you may need to revise part of the plan you have just created. Expect to do this continually because business planning is a *process*.

I founded Powerize.com under the name KnowledgeLink in 1997. The original vision of the company was to furnish a single source of access to internal and external information and provide personalized output. Almost immediately after KnowledgeLink was founded, Yahoo came out with "My Yahoo." While this service was very different from the one KnowledgeLink was offering it had a commoditizing effect on the software we were building. This unforeseen development caused the first revision of our business plan. Shortly thereafter, IBM offered to sell us two content services called IBM InfoMarket and Lotus Newsstand. We made a low bid and, unexpectedly, won. Then less than twelve months from founding the company, we made an acquisition that called for a third business plan revision.

As it happens in launching a venture, we quickly discovered that some of the revenue line items from the IBM InfoMarket acquisition worked better than others. Subscription revenue was working, but pay-per-view for content sales was not. The software side of our business was lagging and Web sites were hot, so we opted to change our name to Powerize.com and put everything under a business information "portal." This called for our fourth business plan rewrite.

At the time, the hottest thing was free content on the Web, supported by ads. We approached some of our major suppliers and negotiated terms for advertiser-driven content sales, causing the fifth business plan rewrite. We filed to go public from this business plan, but when the window quickly shut on dot-com IPOs, we had to turn to the private equity market. We retained Tucker Anthony as our investment banker and they worked with us during the refinement of our sixth business plan. This plan resulted in our negotiation of a merger agreement with Hoovers. Three years and six business plans after founding, we exited into a strategic combination, i.e. merger.

Not all start-up companies are forced to deal with as much chaos as Powerize.com. However, almost all high-potential ventures with a far-reaching horizon will experience a certain amount of chaos during the course of their development. The problem is, when the chaos is occurring, it is difficult to know what's really going on. Chaos brings about the need for creativity and transformation. It is important to sustain your initial vision and horizon, but equally important to allow it to change when changing is necessary. By neglecting to do so, you are ignoring the opportunities for creative openings that eventually lead to innovation.

The Back-of-the-Envelope Business Plan

Every prospective entrepreneur has heard rumors of some lucky entrepreneur who wrote a business plan on the back of an envelope in a cocktail lounge, and then went on to raise a few million from it. This story is part truth and part illusion. The common truth is that thousands of business plans begin as mere sketches. During my early entrepreneurial days, I made dozens of trips to Silicon Valley and I certainly remember having brainstorming discussions while sketching on a cocktail napkin on perhaps every one of those trips. Of course, the illusion is that an entrepreneur can go on to raise millions from the back-of-the-envelope plan without ever writing a complete business plan or assembling a team. Perhaps millions were raised from such plans, but a lot went on between the napkin and the final check.

The common truth is that thousands of business plans begin as mere sketches scribbled on a napkin.

Nonetheless, the cocktail napkin is a great way to jot down ideas as you brainstorm. I highly recommend using a scratch pad of some sort for recording thoughts. All ideas begin somewhere. Ideas that are generated while in discussion with other people are often the most powerful because they have the synergistic effect of multiple minds at work. Some people like to call this collaboration "one plus one equals three." Start with cooperative brainstorming but don't end there.

Positioning the Business Plan

One of the first decisions you will have to make before devising your business plan is how to position your business. Which market segment will you attack? What is your pricing model? What will you offer to your customers? How will this product or service be delivered? And how does all of that compare to what the competition or emerging competition is offering? What is your strategy to win dominance over your niche? Look for an initial positioning that gives you a potentially high payoff and minimal competition early on.

Know your market like the back of your hand. Write that fifty times. Now, what did I just say? In order to develop a business plan, you must first get to know your market segment. Otherwise, you're just wasting time. In earlier chapters I discussed how to learn about your market. Refer to the table for a recap. After that, if you still don't know which market segment to pursue, you may need to repeat this process until you make that decision. Once you have completed this exercise, you have gone a long way towards positioning your business plan.

Understanding the Market

Developing a successful business plan lies in understanding your market and which segment to target with your innovation. Find out which one is the best fit where your competition won't eat you alive and where the demand for your unique strength is the strongest. If you don't already know your market, then how can you get to know it? Here are some tips:

- Attend a trade show in your market, visit with the vendors, and listen to their talks.
- Do as much free research on the Web as you can. Search news sources, Web sites, and publications.
- Get to know the analysts in your field and read some of their reports. Know the numbers cold.
- Visit with the analysts, if possible, and interview them.
- Talk to potential customers to find out their needs and opinions of your new venture concept. Get together with at least half a dozen informed sources.

- Find out who makes buying or spending decisions and learn how and when they do their budgets. Find out who their suppliers are and what competitive products they use.
- Try out some competitive products yourself. Play the role of the user.
- Read about the latest academic research on your technology and find out where it's going and who's funding it.
- Uncover the names of some venture capitalists that fund ventures in your area. Talk to some analysts who work with them to learn as much as you can.
- Talk to potential suppliers and distributors and see what you can learn from them.

One of the best tools for determining the position of your company is the two-axis chart, sometimes called the Magic Quadrant. Market analysts use them all the time. Typically, one axis delineates a range of product or technology sophistication, and the other axis delineates the type of customer, ranging from experts to your average consumers. The chart can be scaled in various ways to perform different analyses. After formatting the scale of your chart, you should plot the location of all the known, significant players in the field. These will mostly be your competitors, but sometimes includes your suppliers and distributors as well. Then, find a good position for your own venture that will enable you to utilize your strengths, but distances you from your competition. You may need to select several different axis scales until you find one that works well for your new venture. As an example, see the chart below and its explanation.

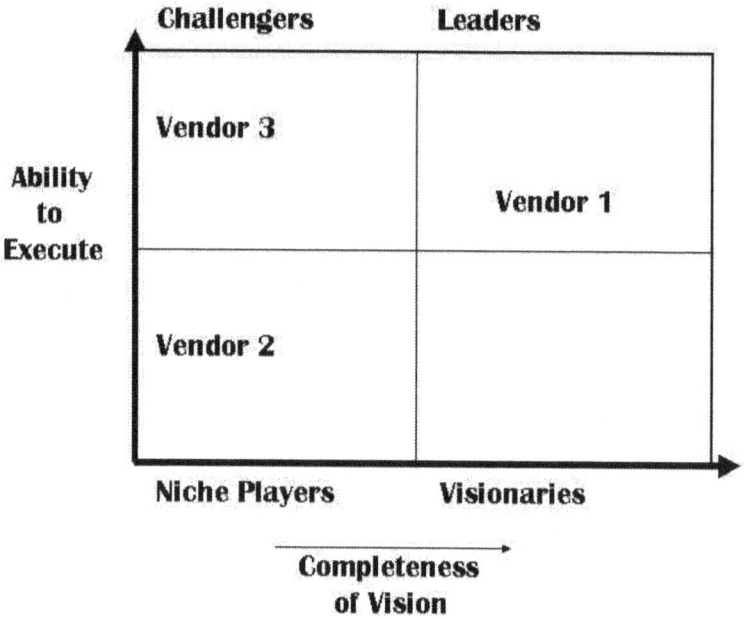

ref: Gartner Group IT Journal, http://gartner11.gartnerweb.com/gg/
static/itjournal/about_mq.html

Determining Your Business Model

Once you know which market segment you want to tackle and where you
might be positioned within that segment as determined by a two-dimen-
sional chart, your business model should become clearer. But what does a
business model mean? A business model is the architecture of your product or service that describes how it meets the needs of customers and generates revenue. In other words, it answers the following questions:

- What are you going to sell?
- To whom?
- Why will they buy it?
- How does it generate revenue?

A business model may follow the traditional format, or it may be a new, revolutionary business model. New business models are the mantra of the Internet, or at least they were before the dot-com meltdown. In *Leading the Revolution*, Gary Hamel suggests that revolutionary new business models are *the* way to position a business for rapid growth. This belief can be true in some cases, but it is not always the formula for success.

There are two vital things that count in a successful venture: 1) making money and 2) sidestepping insurmountable competition.

New business models are risky. You need to have the ability to change quickly if they fail. "Break the rules" was the theme of Internet venturing. But those who violated fundamental rules of business were those who fell the hardest during the dot-com meltdown. A bewildering number of business models were tried, with each model suggesting a different revenue opportunity, such as advertising, subscriptions, transaction fees, direct sales to consumers, and broker fees for matching buyers to sellers. In the end, there are only two things that count in a successful venture: 1) making money and 2) sidestepping insurmountable competition. If these tasks can be done with a revolutionary business model that gains traction in the market, then your model can be a powerful propellant. Let's take a look at a couple examples of business model positioning and explore how their positioning impacted their progress in the market.

A business model is the architecture of your product or service that describes how it meets the needs of customers and generates revenue.

ConQuest was a search engine that accepted natural language queries in plain English and returned the most relevant results based upon word meanings in context, not just keyword matches. The product was positioned as a software product that was sold to diverse markets: online services, providers of information, analysts specializing in intelligence and law enforcement, and large corporations. The customers bought the product because it enabled them to access information with accuracy and ease. The method for obtaining revenue was to charge a perpetual license fee upon the sale, plus an annual maintenance fee for customer support and upgrades.

The ConQuest business model had its advantages and disadvantages. The advantages included the ability to generate revenue quickly on a few large accounts without a significant loss due to marketing costs. A major disadvantage was that ongoing revenue depended mostly upon new sales, as the license fees were much higher than the maintenance fees. Furthermore, the company was vulnerable to competitors who attempted to commoditize the pricing in the market. In fact, in 1994, Verity did just that by developing a new pricing system that undercut the market by about 80 percent. Their price slashing ultimately did not produce enough revenue and they eventually raised prices. But until then, they created havoc in the marketplace in order to gain market share, which was most likely their intent. The market turmoil caused by Verity further pushed ConQuest to the high end of the market, where it enjoyed the ownership of a strong niche. However, it never became a dominant force in the market.

Interestingly enough, while ConQuest, Verity, and other players in the search engine market were engaged in price wars, new market entrants such as Architext (eventually renamed Excite) were entering with completely different business models. Excite, of course, used its search engine to index the Web, provided free searching to consumers, and made its revenue by selling banner advertisements on the search pages. In the end, these companies were in a completely different market for search engines—one that was much more lucrative, at least for a while.

Developing the Business Plan

Business plans have multiple purposes. Most entrepreneurs think of them as proposals to raise capital. Indeed, they are used for that purpose. But how about using a business proposal to run your business? What a novel idea! The plan may also be for securing a loan, convincing a strategic partner to enter into a deal with you, or selling your company. For each of these situations, there are multiple kinds of plans that may be needed: executive summary, financial pro forma, chart presentation, or a full-blown business plan. These needs will come and go constantly. As stated, your business plan will change regularly.

A true business plan is almost like a database management system (DBMS). A DBMS controls the organization, storage, retrieval, security, and integrity of data in a database. It also transfers and accepts new data without disruption to the existing system. I advocate establishing a process to develop the core business plan. At any time, a plan may be needed with a certain specification. The core business plan may be used to generate any of a number of different "reports" for different reasons. Perhaps a line manager needs the operational budget. A banker may want to lend capital and needs to see the pro forma projections, as well as the historical financials. Or perhaps a potential investor wants a two-page executive summary. Such efforts should be drawn from the initial business plan, but perhaps in a different light, depending upon the person for whom the report is being prepared.

The development of the core business plan is an important business operation. It is not something you perform only once a year or so. It is something that needs to be developed continually. A delicate balance needs to be struck between the involvement of you, the CEO, and the inclusion of your staff in modifying the business plan. It is quite important that the staff contribute to this operation.

Eliciting the help of your staff is one of the most valuable management techniques you can deploy. When people help to create the plan, they also take ownership of carrying it out. However, it is very important that the CEO sets the vision for the company and maintains the focus of the business plan on this vision. I suggest that the CEO should point to the long-term objectives and act as the critic, while the rest of the staff figure out the details.

The development of the core business plan is an important business operation. It is not something you perform only once a year or so. It is something that needs to be developed continually.

You should select a core group of management to actively participate in business planning. One suggestion is to hold a few brainstorming meetings. You will discover what the staff thinks the company does and how; what they think the company needs in order to grow; what they believe the company's strengths and weaknesses are; and how they think the company stacks up against its competitors. You may find that everyone in the room has a different idea. By discussing and debating each point you'll bring the team together and hone in on a unified approach.

Business Plan Formats

There are a number of business plan formats that can be used facilitate the drilling down from a high-level vision to a detailed plan of action. With the first couple of steps complete—the back-of-the-envelope plan that summarizes your vision and the determination of your positioning— building a detailed business plan can be attacked.

The PowerPoint Plan

The PowerPoint Plan is what I like to call the rapid prototype of the business plan. First, form an outline of the elements of your business plan and then quickly create some PowerPoint charts that spell out the plan. Try to keep the charts simple with as few words as possible. After you have completed them, share the charts with those people on your business planning team and iterate for them the improved content and details. A criterion to employ: Make certain a layman without explanation can understand each chart.

The PowerPoint Plan is your quick and dirty plan. You can complete it very rapidly even though it may lack details. It can serve as a guide for the continued business planning process. And you can actually use it for those situations that arise before the more complete plan is prepared. Contents of the PowerPoint Plan should include:

- Overview of the business
- Product or service
- Proprietary value
- Targeted market
- Competition
- Business model
- Development milestones
- Sales plan
- Management team
- Financial projection

The Modular Business Plan

The modular business plan is a continuation of the PowerPoint plan. These charts should be more carefully developed and more visual, with pictures and fewer words. The pictures should tell a story and paint the vision.

After the charts have been completed, a modular business plan should have a page of descriptive text for each facing page that is a chart. The text page should describe the business issues in detail and provide assumptions and back-up information, as well as facts of interest. The picture should tell the story visually, but in less detail.

The value of a modular business plan is that it is just plain easy—easy to develop, easy to modify and maintain, easy to tailor to different audience needs quickly, and easy to present and view. To be complete, however, the modular business plan needs to be complemented with a set of financial projections.

The Financial Model

There are many software products and other tools available to help build financial models for business plans. For this task I advocate using software. A good financial model forces you to enter all of the business assumptions into spreadsheet models and then it generates proper profit and loss statements, cash flow statements, and balance sheets. BizPlan Builder and Rhonstadt Financials are two examples of software that can be used for this purpose. Depending upon your needs, you may want to develop your own program.

This part of the business plan should be prepared by your CFO, with input coming from your operational management team. This team of people must live with the numbers once they are finished and, therefore, they should create them. The CEO, of course, has veto authority, and provides the leadership throughout the entire process.

No additional time will be spent on this topic, as there are many other more technical sources to assist in developing a financial model. My parting comment on this subject is that establishing, tracking, and maintaining the financial model should be the basis of your operational budgeting and milestone setting, therefore making it an ongoing business process. This will be important to your long-term effectiveness, as bankers will use the forecasts to provide financing but will use historical data to judge the company's performance.

The Full-Up Business Plan

If you did everything I have suggested thus far, you now possess a cocktail napkin sketch of your business concept, a defined business model, a modular business plan, and a financial model. And, oh yes, you have filled out all ninety-nine forms from Rhonda Abrams's book, *The Successful Business Plan.*

If you are beyond the pure seed stage of your business, you will need a formal business plan, the traditional thirty to fifty pages of written text, for many purposes. The development of such a plan should not be rushed—except for the fact that you need it by yesterday for raising capital! I suggest that you refer to *The Successful Business Plan* and all of the materials it has you prepare in order to develop this plan. This plan will ultimately be encapsulated into one front-to-back document. The executive summary, the two-page summary of the entire plan, is particularly important, as it will be used time and again for many different purposes.

Every book, article, or chapter on business planning contains an outline of the necessary components of a good business plan. Rather than repeat this practice, I have instead included a chart that relates certain sections of the business plan to how they will probably be interpreted by those evaluating you based upon this plan. This exercise should give you some perspective when it comes to deciding which factors to address in your plan.

Business Plan Section	What is conveyed?
Executive Summary	• Is it obvious what this business is about? • Is the market opportunity compelling? • Is the business going to be large?
Company Overview	• Is the company real and established? • How big is the company and where is it located? • What is the background of the principles?

Product Section	• What is the product or service being offered? • What stage of development is it in? • What is the proprietary value?
Market Section	• Is the market real and large? • Does the entrepreneur understand the market? • Is there sufficient room for this venture to succeed?
Competition	• Is the entrepreneur aware of the competition? • Is there a market lead or niche to play in? • Can the competition be beaten?
Management Team	• Has the team been partially established? • Does the team have experience and past successes? • What additional resources are needed?
Operational Milestones	• Does the entrepreneur have realistic goals? • In what stage is the company? • What needs to be accomplished?
Financial Projections	• How does the entrepreneur think? • How does this way of thinking compare to public comparables? • Are the projections within believable ranges?
Investment and Use of Proceeds	• How much money is being sought? • For what is it needed? • What is the valuation expectation?

Before going on to discuss presenting the business plan, I will reiterate and summarize a few thoughts on the plan and its meaning:

- Remember that the business plan is a compass, not a roadmap. It will point you in the right direction, but in order to make it work, feedback and management are required.
- Things will not always go according to the plan. There are no failures, only quitters. Stick to it!
- The corridor principal is very real. Starting a venture is like walking down a long corridor in the hopes of finding a light at the end. Along the way there are doors, sometimes to other corridors. On occasion, you may decide to take one of the doors instead of staying in your original corridor. When this happens, you will need to adapt your business plan.

The modular business plan, well-written executive summary, and financial model will be the core business plan assets to maintain.

I recommend that you begin with the back-of-the-envelope business plan, business model, and PowerPoint business plan, and then gradually evolve those into the modular business plan. Later, the modular business plan, well-written executive summary, and financial model will be the core business plan assets to maintain. These should be updated no less often than quarterly. From there, you may compile these into a full-up business plan twice per year.

Presenting the Business Plan

In the life of a venture, the business plan will not only constantly change, but it will constantly be presented to many different audiences. Such audiences will include potential investors as well as strategic partners, large customers, prospective employees, current staff, shareholders, analysts,

bankers, and possibly suppliers and distributors as well. The value underlying the modular business plan format is that you can quickly tailor the
presentation to suit various audiences while maintaining the core business
plan.

Analyze your audience. To whom are you presenting? What will catch
their attention? After considering these aspects, choose a subset of your
charts and a flow that matches the needs of your audience.

Suppose that you are presenting your business plan to a prospective
angel investor. A knowledgeable angel is far more tolerant and understanding than a wealthy relative who will get angry if your venture fails.
The angel can help more than either a relative or a distant venture capitalist. Present to angels who have done it before. Informal "get to know you"
formats are usually best. These angels are looking for chemistry and fun,
not just a prospectus. Your presentation to an angel might be a casual
chart "flip through" in a lounge, displayed during a candid conversation
with nothing held back.

On the other hand, if you must present to a venture capitalist, you
want to prepare for a more formal presentation. Be succinct. These people
are impatient, busy, and overworked. They are looking for uniqueness,
management, projections, and a planned exit. It is vitally important that
you play in a market space that they understand and like. The presentation should be straightforward and honest. Make sure everything you say
is true without error of omission. There is no faster way to lose credibility.
Show that you can sell by your style, but don't be arrogant. The subject of
venture capital will be explored in more detail in Chapter 8.

At all times, you should have with you a brief, impromptu, six-chart
overview. Furthermore, you will want to have an "elevator speech" well-
prepared and ready for frequent use. An elevator speech is an overview
that can be delivered on an elevator ride to a walk-in sales opportunity.
Comprised of only a couple sentences, it should capture the single most
important thing that you do, your vision, and your benefits. It should be
very compact, simple, and understandable. You must be able to deliver it

powerfully, enthusiastically, and flawlessly. An effective elevator speech can be used numerous times a day to sell your vision, your product, and your company for investment or to prospective employees. After all, if you are the founder/CEO, then you are the best salesman and this is merely one of your tools.

With your business plan in hand, along with your ability to communicate it, you are truly ready. You have the compass, so now it's time to prepare the execution of your plan. Let's then move onward to the next chapter, about "sharpening your ax"!

Chapter 5

Sharpening the Ax

"If I had eight hours to chop down a cherry tree,
I would spend six hours sharpening my ax."
—Abraham Lincoln

"Sharpening the Ax" refers to a period of incubation for your venture. During this time you will prepare to implement your strategy, develop early alliances, establish connections to secure beta test sites, and complete early prototypes. All of these things must be done before launching a major market penetration effort. Appropriating a generous amount of time for preparation will ultimately result in a stronger and more focused entry into the market. In this chapter, we will address beta sites, reference accounts, strategic partners, and product readiness, among myriad tasks that need to be undertaken in order to prepare for market penetration.

Sharpening the Ax

Your idea is in hand, your horizon is defined, your early team is aboard, you have a first draft of your business plan complete, and your product development is under way. However, it is too soon to start penetrating the market. So what should be done at this point? As the famous quote from

Abraham Lincoln goes, "If I had eight hours to chop down a cherry tree, I would spend six hours sharpening my ax." While it may not yet be time for you to chop, it *is* time to sharpen your ax. But how do you sharpen your ax? Executing several of the following tasks will prepare your venture for market launch:

- Find beta sites and early prospects willing to test your product.
- Secure strategic relationships with larger companies.
- Make your product market-ready as opposed to only developing the core technology.
- Land first customers and reference accounts.
- Brief industry analysts and allow them to influence your product.
- Benchmark product performance.
- Develop marketing materials.

In 1999, when I was CEO of Powerize.com, we made a run at the wacky IPO market for dot-coms. By all traditional measures, Powerize.com was not ready for an IPO. However, the capital markets in 1999 enabled almost any partially established Internet company to go public. We acquired a round of private capital from a public company in upstate New York and the major usage of proceeds for that round was used to "sharpen the ax" for our forthcoming public offering. The IPO was unsuccessful, as the market window closed before the SEC completed a final review of our documents. However, this seemingly unfortunate event worked to our benefit in the long run. You will read about all the reasons not to do an early IPO in Chapter 9. But for now, let's discuss how Powerize.com used the pre-IPO round to sharpen the ax.

...it was most definitely the "sharp ax" that enabled the growth to happen.

Powerize.com launched its Web site and Internet service, a business research portal for consumers and business managers, in April 1999. At its launch the product was a retooling of the IBM Infomarket service with an editorial flair. The professional information was not free, which was somewhat unacceptable at that time in the Internet world. Powerize.com closed on a $5 million round at that time. In order to sharpen its ax, we decided to do the following within ninety days:

- Re-launch the service free of cost to its users, with advertising and sponsorships as the primary business model.
- Transform the search engine from a privately licensed software tool to a major brand name on the Internet.
- Become affiliated with at least one major Internet portal.
- Add three more strategic alliances.
- Sign a major advertising agency and an ad sales agency.

As we drafted our S1 registration form for the SEC in the ninety days that followed, Powerize.com performed some heroic measures. We closed deals with high-profile Internet players including major suppliers to Lexis Nexis and Dialog (primary traditional online services that charge a fee for content), Inktomi, two New York ad agencies, and Netscape, VerticalNet, and NBC. In addition, Powerize.com had established itself with a major industry analyst in Boston, causing our company to be favorably cited in numerous industry reports and conference talks.

Despite the fact that the Powerize.com IPO did not happen, the next four quarters showed revenue going from $300,000 per quarter to just under $1.5 million per quarter, as a result of the steady increases in traffic and revenue. However, this result did not come about without going through a lot of growing pain first. Powerize.com faced both heavy cash flow pressure and severe difficulties in managing engineers during this period. We utilized those ninety days to our utmost advantage to prepare for our next round of funding. Ultimately, it was most definitely the sharp ax that enabled the company's growth to happen.

Establishing Early Adopter and Beta Partners

One type of reader I hope this book will benefit is the first-time entrepreneur so he or she can avoid some of the pitfalls that have snared others.

One tendency that I have seen repeated time and again by first-time entrepreneurs, including myself, is the inclination to sell the product immediately following the launch. After a successful launch, a wave of euphoria spreads over the new company because the first positive results have emerged from the prototyping efforts in the laboratories. The new entrepreneur then instantly proceeds to establish a sales force and sell the product. This zealousness has to be applauded. However, you must distinguish between the kinds of selling that should occur now. At this time sales should be focused on selling the concept to the early adopters. Mainstream product sales must occur later with a professional sales force. As the entrepreneur or founder, early sales is your job.

The first step after producing results on the prototype bench is to seek early adopter prospects and beta test sites. As potential customers who are willing to test your product, these companies are extremely valuable assets. For this reason, you should not charge early adopters a fee until you have delivered real business benefits. But you should plan a method to convert betas into paying customers—an important benchmark. For now, these companies are doing you a huge favor. Securing their buy-in is crucial to the evolution of your product or service. It is vital that you secure the financing necessary to enable you to take this step. Avoid the common urge to do a rocket blastoff too soon. It will kill you! The pressure to achieve may prompt you into moving too quickly. You need to balance between the two extremes—moving too quickly and not at all.

ConQuest benefited greatly from the assistance of early adopter customers that tested our product. As an SBIR government-funded venture, ConQuest was close to its public sector customers. Various government intelligence agencies became early adopters of the ConQuest search engine. These agencies had a multitude of power-user requirements and they wanted to license ConQuest because of the product's superior accuracy. However, the agencies often had access to funds for licensing, but not for development. In order to solve this dilemma, ConQuest licensed its search engine to some customers sooner than they were ready for it and used the cash from the license fee to build out the power-user features that the customers wanted.

You must distinguish between selling to early adopters and mainstream product sales.

ConQuest's second market was comprised of publishers and online services. Infonautics was one of our first customers in this area. ConQuest built the features that Infonautics needed in return for accelerated license fees. ConQuest's transition to full-blown sales in the commercial marketplace was a little more difficult, and it required some outside financing from Motorola New Enterprises. After a few fits with our sales force, which have been discussed, ConQuest stabilized sales under a very successful VP of Sales.

Although it is obviously beneficial to attract early adopters, the process of courting them needs careful management. Those that are intolerant of late-stage development are poor choices as early adopter and beta test candidates. Once early adopters have signed on, it's important to balance "feature creep"—or constant product updates from the engineers adding new features—and your product release schedule. This is not an easy task when customers are allowed to request new features in your product. This privilege should be reserved only for the early and very best customers. Otherwise, you risk that the product may never become stable enough to be sold in high volume.

It takes a very unique type of sales person to sell products at a conceptual level before the product actually exists. Do not confuse this type of sales with majority market selling. While at ConQuest, I enacted my sales force too soon. This poor decision resulted in a period of time when I continued to make most of the sales, while the new sales force floundered. Why did this happen? As mentioned earlier, I was selling the company vision and the concept for the product, acquiring early adopter customers who believed in the vision and were encouraged by my enthusiasm. The sales force was selling a tool in a box that they couldn't fully offer yet.

Hence, their approach had a low success rate until the product matured. This mistake can be frustrating and very costly and can be avoided if conceptual sales are consciously planned.

A responsibility that comes with the privilege of acquiring an early adopter customer is to balance your utopian vision with steadfast execution. Overselling the vision and under-delivering the product will soon cause a loss in your company's credibility. I experienced this unfortunate situation at Powerize.com, where the business development staff was promising products with new features built-in, rather than products containing off-the-shelf features. This misunderstanding created an unmanageable engineering burden that was only resolved through burnout levels of overtime work. The problem could have been avoided by limiting the authority of the business development staff. Execution and balance are required disciplines when pre-selling products.

Managing Cash during the Sharpening Period

Time for guerilla tactics. Your revenue will be scanty and your development expenses will be at an all-time high during this period. Regardless of how you are financed, the sharpening period is the time to strive for maximum output while conserving cash. Not only will this tactic help you avoid burning through your cash too quickly, but also it will instill good habits that may last a long time. Similarly, companies that are overcapitalized at this point tend to develop very poor spending habits, rationalizing their behavior by thinking that faster spending will enable them to beat the competition. Faster spending may indeed eliminate competition—it'll take you out of the race completely.

We practiced good spending habits at ConQuest during our sharpening period in 1991–1992. ConQuest was founded during a recession and bootstrapped its first three years of existence. We were abruptly thrown into the early adopter customer phase when we met the cofounder of Physicians Online at an artificial intelligence trade show. Wanting to achieve superior searching for his customers, he wanted our product faster than we were able to deliver it. Physicians Online had a very large database of medical texts. It not only required a large index and fast access for lots of simultaneous unsophisticated users (i.e. doctors), but it also needed a specialized vocabulary to perform at its best. ConQuest was able to obtain SBIR funding from the National Institute of Health to build a medical online dictionary based upon their existing vocabulary sets. This was immediately turned into a commercial product in a royalty-bearing deal.

During this period, there were half a dozen occasions when funding came from a different source and each time the company was very well-disciplined in producing a lot on a small amount of cash. Doing so is one of the long-term benefits of properly managing early adopter and beta test customers.

Landing Strategic Partners

The most overused word in the history of business literature is the word strategic. And the most overused application of that word is strategic partner. What are strategic partners anyway? And why are they necessary?

Let's start by stating what a strategic partner is *not*. A strategic partner is not simply a customer, beta test site, or reference account. Nor is it a supplier or distributor, unless the relationship is more complex than that. The two words in strategic partner both hold a special significance to the meaning of the phrase.

Take the second word: partner. A partner is someone with whom you collaborate to do business. Partners are equals at some level. Each partner must contribute something for the partnership to be mutually beneficial. That means that both members of the partnership have to put forth effort. Both parties benefit from the partnership because one contributes some resource or service that would normally be difficult or expensive for the other to obtain.

A strategic partner is a person with whom you collaborate in order to accomplish something vital to the success of your business. This task must be one that is on a direct, critical path to your horizon.

Now for the elusive, overused strategic. A strategic partner is one with whom you collaborate in order to accomplish something vital to the success of your business, and who helps you achieve goals beyond incremental revenue. The partners you select must lie on a direct, critical path to your horizon. You do not have the time and energy for too many partnerships, and therefore you can only afford to work with those who are directly in synch with your focus. Remember, put all the wood behind the arrow.

Scouting for Partners

Where should you look for strategic partners? Look into every source within your reach. Here are a few ideas:

- Referrals from your advisors and board of directors
- Professional and industry organizations
- Referrals from your accountant and lawyer
- Industry trade shows
- Cold calls in Silicon Valley (really!)

Silicon Valley has a refreshingly no-nonsense, yet laid-back attitude, but they get down to business quickly.

I cannot over-emphasize the nature of business in Silicon Valley. I recall a time when I was traveling to the Valley with the CEO of Excalibur with the intention of drumming up new business partners. Our calendars were only about half full, if that, and sometimes the scheduled meetings ended earlier than planned. Often, we would pull out our cell phones and organizers while driving up and down Highway 101 and start making phone calls asking for appointments of opportunity. It usually only took about fifteen minutes to be granted a walk-in appointment, and about one-third of these meetings produced some kind of result. Silicon Valley has a refreshingly no nonsense, yet laid-back attitude. The people there know that out-of-towners have limited time during their visits, so they grant meetings rather easily. On the other hand, and to the good of both parties, they cut to the chase very quickly, usually in the first few minutes of the meeting. That's business American style—but don't try it on the East Coast unless you are circling Boston on Route 128.

During the launch of my ventures, I always made a habit of visiting Silicon Valley once every month or two. Typically, I would take an early seven o'clock flight, land at ten o'clock in San Francisco, attend four to five meetings throughout the day and evening, another six to seven meetings the following day, and then take a red-eye home. Twelve meetings in two days—a prime example of making the best use of your time and money during this ax-sharpening period. I once had a VP working for me at ConQuest who would take one day to fly to Silicon Valley, one day for a single meeting, and the next day to fly home. This blatant wasting of time made me absolutely crazy. Needless to say, he was not around for long.

Obviously, there are many other ways to find strategic partners besides roaming around Silicon Valley. And I most certainly am not suggesting that searching the Valley is the primary way to operate. But it is fun and educational and it builds self-confidence. If you are in a high-tech business, it is worth the time and expense. And if your business is located in Silicon Valley, you have no excuse for not getting out and frequently working the field.

After using your network to find candidates for strategic partners, it is always smart to check references. Talk to those that have worked with your potential partners. In addition, you should research the organizations with which your candidates are affiliated and evaluate how well they fit with your mission and horizon. Lastly, take your time to negotiate carefully. Don't settle for the wrong partner or the wrong agreement simply to become associated with a name or grab a few bucks.

Setting Silicon Valley aside, wouldn't it be ideal to have your strategic partner in your own backyard? Often in the quest for a high-profile partner we forget to consider potential partners that are close to home. In its early days, ConQuest succeeded in attracting resellers by advertising in *Washington Technology*, which was near the location of our headquarters. We received several calls from potential partners each time we advertised.

Of course, advertising also exposes you to your competition. One of the most unusual experiences I had during ConQuest's beta test phase was a call I received in response to one of our ads seeking beta sites. Our ad had claimed that we had created an accurate, scalable, natural language search engine. The call that I just mentioned came from the CEO of one of our soon to be head-to-head competitors. He had spotted the ad and called me to say that I should not even bother to build our product because he had already done so. When he introduced himself, I didn't recognize who he was and he responded, "Don't you know who I am?" I said no and he replied, "I am a pioneer in the field of text retrieval!" And then he proceeded to tell me why ConQuest would never make it with his company as competition. This phone call became a standing joke at ConQuest. Ultimately, we did compete with this CEO's company. We won some, lost some, and eventually we overtook them. Our ultimate exit came at four times their price. It pays to not be intimidated by the arrogance of your competitors.

Don't forget the beauty of public relations. If you haven't done so already, now is the time to raise your profile in the industry through a baseline public relations initiative. Send press releases to your industry trade publications with news of recent hires, product development milestones that have been reached, or any other newsworthy material. Doing so may bring a great partner to you.

Referrals, Silicon Valley, your backyard—where else can you find partners? Another way to obtain partnerships is to buy them. This method became popular in the greedy era of dot-coms. You could secure a partnership for a mere annual "slotting fee" of several hundred thousand dollars, or maybe several million to ensure your product is positioned within a partner's portfolio. Buying partnerships is the way in which the Internet industry manufactured circular revenue, inflated its profit and loss statements, and did early public offerings. For example, Company A pays Company B a slotting fee, who pays Company C a license fee, who pays Company D a slotting fee, who buys a subscription from Company A. Of course, Companies A, B, C, and D were all funded by the same venture capitalist. The auditors could not keep up with such bartered circular revenue, so they all booked it and went public. Then came the bust.

That said, it is not *always* a bad idea to buy a partnership. This practice is not a very common one in the dot-com world anymore, but it may be to your advantage in unique cases. However, you must recognize that buying a partner is not necessarily developing a true partnership. You are merely becoming someone's customer.

Another technique for obtaining partnerships is to buy them. This method became popular in the greedy era of dot-coms. You could secure a partnership for a mere annual slotting fee.

Powerize.com "bought" several of its key relationships with investment dollars. Some, but not all of these purchases, turned out to be smart moves. The most significant one was an alliance developed with a major aggregator of business publications. It turned out that this aggregator supplied to all of the subscription-based services like Lexis Nexis. Powerize.com's objective was to offer the same content on the Internet for free, and eventually we did. Our free service wreaked havoc across the industry for quite some time. We had to pay a seven-figure price for this content partnership, but in our case it created a new business model in the traditional publishing industry. Powerize.com has since been sold to Hoovers, a company that chose to focus on subscription revenue as the advertising world collapsed.

Choosing the Right Partner

Choosing the right partner is a very critical task. Who is the right partner? Assess your needs and focus on locating a partner who can offer the resources you are unable to supply. Also, conduct an analysis of the market sectors and customers most important to your company. Identify those with the most opportunity and seek a partner who can assist you in targeting those areas.

A partnership, if successful, has the potential to become a long-term win-win relationship. It is important to listen to your intuition about the partners with whom you are considering developing alliances. Can you work with them? What are their intents? Are they likely to stick to their plan or be blown by the wind? What do you expect to get out of this strategic partnership? Do they have lots of money? Do they have a business need for what you offer? I have often seen start-up companies partner with other start-ups. For the most part, this partnership does not make sense. Start-ups have too many needs, change direction too often, and have a high failure rate. Larger, more stable entities are likely to be around and they may have a need for the technology you are developing.

You must also assess what you are willing to sacrifice for the partnership. Large companies will often seek to have an exclusive right to your technology. In the long haul, exclusive partnerships are very limiting, but in the short-term, such exclusivity can be very beneficial to you. The key to working with a partner who seeks exclusivity in a given market segment is to tie this right to revenue performance and put a time limit on the terms.

ConQuest held a corporate partnership with Motorola in its early days. At the time, Motorola was launching a new venture to provide online information services. The company needed ConQuest's search engine. Likewise, we needed Motorola as a source of cash and as a beta test site with a recognized customer who would put our product to a scalability test. ConQuest licensed its products to Motorola for the new enterprise. In trade, ConQuest received a handsome license fee and an equity investment from Motorola. Additionally, Motorola used the ConQuest product extensively and provided valuable feedback. Company representatives sat on our board of directors and advised us about our business. They loaned money to us when we hit a cash crunch. Unfortunately, Motorola's new business venture was discontinued, but not until well after ConQuest had reaped the necessary benefits. In return, Motorola also made a nice profit on its investment in ConQuest.

As an example of how partners are not always compatible, I will tell you about two different government contractors with whom ConQuest formed partnerships. One was a diverse technology company located in upstate New York, and the other was a large systems integration company located in Texas. Both companies were resellers of ConQuest's product and they made offers to invest in ConQuest for majority control. These offers were both made at unreasonably low prices, especially in comparison to what the market would bear at the time. Neither partnership panned out and both consumed a lot of time. Trust was never built between the companies. In retrospect, we concluded that the needs of government contractors are very different from those of the typical commercial enterprise with which we dealt. Government contractors have a high need for exclusivity, they are very cash-driven, and they like to do things as inexpensively as possible. Conversely, commercial enterprises usually seek access to technology to support a product launch or competitive position.

We steadfastly avoided exclusivity in our relationships and remained very open about our "no exclusivity" policy. It often cost us sales to larger enterprises in our early days but, in the end, we would not have been able to negotiate a merger with Excalibur if we had been bound by exclusive relationships.

On one occasion, there was an Air Force RFP for an accurate text retrieval solution. Nine different system integrators contacted us to bid. Among system integrators were the two partners mentioned previously. Instead of only bidding to provide the text retrieval solution for one of the system integrators, we opted to bid non-exclusively on all nine teams. This plan worked for us, mainly because we clearly had the best technology to meet the government's need. For this project we partnered with a small company in Buffalo called Calspan. This agreement made another partner in upstate New York that had lost the deal fuming mad. But we politely reminded them that we did not operate under exclusive partnerships.

This incident vividly illustrates the tradeoff involved in partnering exclusively versus non-exclusively. It is a choice every company must make, but one that you must make very consciously when working with corporate partners.

Managing the Partnership

Landing your first strategic partner can be an exhilarating experience and can lead to a feeling of pending success. This milestone is always a strong confidence builder and you should pause to enjoy it. But recognize that the real work is about to begin. Managing a strategic partnership is hard work. The adage that you only get out of it what you put into it applies. In this case, you only get out of it what you *both* put into it.

When crafting your partnership agreements, it is important to set reasonable limits on your contributions. There are plenty of people who will take advantage if you allow it. You must make it clear from the beginning what you will do for free, what you will do for a fee, and what you will not do at all. Your partner should define their parameters as well.

Because your partner will have its own needs and expectations, it is not a good idea to form strategic partnerships with other start-ups. ConQuest partnered with a start-up imaging company. The company paid us $5,000 for software and then continually asked for integration, training, and development work, all because they had paid the first license fee. Small start-up companies lack resources and sometimes seek to obtain them however they can. The only possible exception to partnering with another start-up is if you are licensing a completed product and there's no threat of constant modifications.

You should also be cautioned about dealing with government contracts. One of ConQuest's methods of obtaining quick government cash was to sell a license in lieu of a service contract and then do the service work gratis. This system avoided procurement delays, but often we did not know exactly how much work we would be asked to do for that license, and sometimes the customer expected way more than we had planned.

You will not always have control of the partnership you have to manage. This is especially true when losing a contact person or if your partner company is acquired. Powerize.com had an exceptional relationship with Netscape and had crafted a very good deal for promoting its content on Netcenter. Just before AOL acquired Netscape, the product manager with whom we had dealt quit his job at Netscape. When AOL took over, they no idea what we negotiated and they wanted to change all the terms. It took us about twelve months of a compromised relationship and renegotiations to finally devise a deal that was agreeable to both parties. This turn of events is obviously not what we had planned when we began our business relationship with Netscape. This example highlights the importance of documenting the terms of your relationship where applicable. When the initial deal is complete, take the time to work it through the partner's organization. Make it visible to senior management at several levels.

Strategic partners can help to develop, distribute, or provide needed components for your product. These are your primary objectives in forming alliances. Your partner has other objectives that you must manage and meet. And all of this must be done while maintaining a balance in your company. It is easy to be completely consumed by your partnerships and never get your product to market. Hence, our next subject.

Getting Your Product Ready for Market

Does your engineering team know what a product is? That might sound like an absurd question, but first let's take a moment to understand the nature of the beast. Engineers are among the most intelligent and most needed people in a high tech venture. They are intellectually motivated and like to build cool things. But at the same time, it can be an enormous challenge to bring them to understand marketing needs. Indeed, many of them feel that the merits of the technology alone warrant a product being built.

Almost every high-tech company has to deal with this engineering versus marketing syndrome. ConQuest was no exception. We had a superb search engine, but we could not build a user interface. We tried a Windows interface, a Macintosh interface, and a Web interface. They were all very poor and did not illustrate the outstanding capabilities of our search engine. When we attempted to build a user interface group, it failed due to antagonism between engineering and marketing. We conceded to our limitations and worked around them. Sometimes it is necessary to focus on the select things you do well. Ultimately, we decided to license only the engine and ignore the task of developing an interface. This decision enabled the company to grow faster in the short-term, but it cost us enormously in market capitalization and caused us to miss a major Internet opportunity.

A similar situation occurred at Powerize.com. The company had constructed a successful Web site. It had marketing appeal because we used an outside agency to design the look and feel of the site itself. However, outside of the Web site, Powerize was constantly challenged to develop a stable product set. There were two products that were forever in beta test.

One was a corporate portal server and the other was a content syndication tool for affiliates. The major reason these products were moving targets was that the engineering staff did not understand the user and they were not open to receiving input from marketing. The engineering-marketing syndrome was a constant management battle at Powerize. We had plans to remove certain staff positions and restructure, but we constantly focused on raising money and never fully caught up with the problem. The company grew based upon its Web site business. Advertising, sponsorship, and subscription revenues grew rapidly, but software license fees languished due to the problems described above. Once again, a small company cannot be all things to all people. We focused our energy on what we could do well.

Engineers are among the most intelligent and most needed people in a high tech venture. But at the same time, it can be an enormous challenge to bring them to understand marketing needs.

The engineering versus marketing syndrome can manifest itself in other ways. Consider a former small internet security firm in Palo Alto, CA called GuardOne.com. This firm was funded through an angel round arranged by venture capital investment banker Garage Technology Ventures. GuardOne.com had a staff of seven people who built several Internet filtering software products that were rules based, meaning that users could establish their own rules for the method of content filtration. These products were superbly developed, well engineered, stable, and accompanied by a solid user interface. Upon completion, GuardOne was unable to sell its products. The company was undercapitalized and the market for Internet filtering had long since been established. They had missed their opportunity. Had the company been more in tune with the market, they could have redirected sooner. The company repositioned to another area of Internet security. This mishap is an example of how poor market timing, despite the development of a good, focused product, will most always lead to failure.

How does a venture address difficult issues such as balancing engineering and marketing and ensuring product timing is accurate? One is a cultural issue and the other is a product management issue. With some careful forethought and managerial effort, bad market timing and the engineering-marketing syndrome can easily be avoided. Consider the following suggestions:

- Place a product manager in charge of product specs and release authority. Product management is essential and it must be established from the very start.
- Make product management a marketing function, not an engineering function. A good product manager is a marketing person who understands technology. Often they are engineers by initial training who have migrated to marketing.
- The product manager must be in charge. Everyone, including the engineers, must understand this from the start. Those who can't accept it must be asked to leave. No exceptions.

There is no substitute for a good product manager. It is up to the product manager to monitor the market, know the user, manage schedules and specs, avoid instabilities in product releases, oversee testing, and make the final call on all product releases. The product manager must see that configuration management is maintained in a disciplined manner and that proper alpha and beta testing is never circumvented.

It is up to the founder, or CEO, i.e. you, to leverage both the engineer's and the marketer's strengths and apply them to your vision. This duty has to be performed consciously—otherwise your venture will suffer. The inability to blend engineering technology and marketing insight affects even the most talented of engineers. At ConQuest, the brilliance of the product was, hands down, the artwork of our CTO and cofounder, Paul

Nelson. But along with his brilliance came an enormous focus on the server product along with a reluctance to embrace user interfaces and the Internet. At Powerize.com, the lead engineers were very talented but they did not subscribe to our business vision. Consequently, they were unwilling to convert the content service to a new indexing engine.

Why is it that brilliant engineers sometimes resist good, practical business decisions? Part of the answer lies in understanding their point of view. Engineers are scientifically motivated. They seek intellectual challenges and they worship the elegance of a tough solution. I recently listened to a pitch by an entrepreneur/engineer who was trying to seek funding for his company. He had some really snappy speech technology but did not target a clearly identifiable market. He kept cajoling me to invest because his technology would command "five-million-dollar site licenses." This engineer clearly needed a marketer as a partner to first position his product and then design it for that market prior to pricing it.

Occasionally, a good business decision will compromise the engineer's artistic beauty. A business solution calls for something that is less than elegant or not the most advanced. At ConQuest, user interfaces were considered child's play compared to the elegance of the search engine server that had artificial intelligence embedded within. At Powerize, Inktomi was viewed by the engineers as an inferior search engine, despite the fact that it carried high traffic, high bandwidth, and the respect of the major industry players.

You have a challenge before you. Your challenge is to successfully manage your entire team to produce good business solutions, especially your engineers since they are vital to your operations. This task can be accomplished, but you must respect your engineering staff's intellect and their desire to reason. You must also build respect for marketing. If you cannot successfully perform these duties, you are the wrong CEO for the company, or you have the wrong engineering staff.

An amusing incident occurred at ConQuest between my founding partner and me with our first major commercial software delivery. Paul stayed up all night to complete a project for delivery the next day. When I arrived at work the next morning, I found the delivery disks in an envelope with *handwritten* labels. I went berserk! My marketing side told me to put a professionally printed label on it to at least cast the illusion that we were making deliveries on a regular basis. However, Paul felt that the customer would surely appreciate the fact that he had stayed up all night for them and, therefore, the envelope didn't need a label.

Why is it that brilliant engineers sometimes resist good, practical business decisions? Part of the answer lies in understanding their point of view.

After you have attempted to regulate the battle between engineers and marketers, how will you know when your product is actually ready for market? The ideal answer: When your product manager says so. The real answer: When your product can be used more effectively and productively than its alternatives, and when it is polished and non-annoying to the users. Your product does not yet need to be perfect. But you must have users who are willing to not only buy it—but who use it regularly and are anticipating upgrades and new versions. That is key. Product usage is what you must monitor and strive to achieve.

Of course, it is to your distinct advantage if you are undoubtedly better than your competition in some important respect. If not, your struggles will be many. You must find a way to prove that your product is superior to all others of its kind—through outside third-party endorsements if possible. ConQuest was able to use a government benchmark event to prove this point as described in the box below.

ConQuest and TREC

ConQuest's hallmark to success was a scalable and much more accurate search engine than those developed by its competitors. Accuracy was a difficult concept to explain to prospective buyers and oftentimes they did not properly evaluate this aspect of the product before making a purchase decision. In search engine accuracy performance, there are two measures to consider: precision and recall. Precision is the percentage of hits that are truly relevant. Recall is the percentage of relevant hits that are found.

Fortunately for us, and due to the importance and elusiveness of the accuracy concept, the National Institute of Standards (NIST) began a conference in the early 1990s called TREC, or Text Retrieval Evaluation Conference. This annual event was an accuracy benchmarking, or competition, among many different systems, both research and commercial. One of ConQuest's advisors was a former program manager from the industry-acclaimed Defense Advanced Research Projects Agency. He strongly advised us to participate in TREC to demonstrate the superiority of our system.

In the first year of this competition, ConQuest won, hands down. It was the highest composite average score on a precision-recall curve of all thirty systems that were evaluated. In fact, ConQuest participated for several years in TREC and always came out in the top two or three systems, often as the winner.

The TREC victory was the single most important event in the evolution of ConQuest. It landed us several six- and seven-figure accounts in both government and industry. This victory eventually led to our successful $33-million merger with Excalibur in 1995.

ConQuest touted its success in a press release and was severely slapped on the wrist by NIST. Their claim was that TREC was research and not just a contest. Their new rules were that participants could make no public claims — if they did, they would not be able to participate again. The truth of the matter was, the government feared the loss of funding for TREC by being seen as merely a benchmarking event. It was clearly easier to ask for forgiveness than permission, so I made the decision to heavily promote our results. We were disparaged by some of the other participants for doing so, most notably by the second-place performer, a large Fortune 500 company. However, this price was a very small one to pay.

Interestingly, several of our prime commercial competitors refused to participate or submit their results to TREC. These better-established players had a lot to lose by exposing that their search engines were less accurate than those emerging on the horizon were. ConQuest used this fact in its sales efforts. As a result, buyers often concluded that we had the most accurate search engine on the market at the time.

Establishing Reference Accounts

In *Crossing the Chasm*, Geoffrey Moore discusses the value of reference accounts. Reference accounts enable and accelerate sales in the same market as buyers talk to each other and recommend or warn against certain products. Having a highly visible company as a reference account will compound the positive or negative effects.

Technology enthusiasts will typically reference early stage markets whereas mainstream buyers in the same vertical market will reference later stage markets. This difference leads to the "chasm" effect that Moore's much-acclaimed book addresses so thoroughly. The chasm is the middle market stage between technology enthusiasts and mainstream buyers.

Technology enthusiasts are no longer the key buyers because the technology is not new anymore. Safety-seeking mainstream buyers shy away because the product is still too new and the company is not well established. The chasm is what must be crossed in the transition from one type of buyer to the other. Many high-tech companies fall into oblivion trying to cross this chasm.

Technology enthusiasts will typically reference early stage markets whereas mainstream buyers in the same vertical market will reference later stage markets. This deviation leads to the "chasm" effect that Moore's much-acclaimed book addresses so thoroughly.

In the diagram below, the first two silos under the bell-shaped curve can be thought of as the market of technology enthusiasts and early adopters. The next three silos on the other side of the chasm can be thought of as the early majority market, the mainstream market, and the laggard market. Each of these markets is characterized by the kind of buyer that is present when the venture or product is at that stage of maturity. Technology enthusiasts always come first. They reference each other across industries because their main interest is technology. The early adopters are similar, but they are more interested in the product than the technology. But because they tend to buy everything new, they too reference each other across industries.

Now, the early majority buyer is the least conservative of buyers in general. These people are buying products for a business purpose, but they are not completely risk averse. They reference each other only within their vertical industry. This type of referencing brings about the chasm in high-tech companies. In the early stages of a product, high-tech companies have a tendency to market horizontally because it is the most efficient way to reach the early adopters. But when the tide shifts, there is a sudden lack of references because the previous buyers are scattered across many different industries and they don't consult with each other at the majority buyer level, where business need is the main concern.

As I said earlier, you, the entrepreneur, are the primary sales person for technology enthusiasts, early adopters, and the first reference accounts. As indicated by the curve in the diagram below, the first reference accounts are technology enthusiasts that reference each other. But the reference accounts you eventually need to drive a growing sales force are early majority reference accounts. They are essential to close deals. You can obtain early majority reference accounts by drawing upon your early adopter customers that may appear to be early majority as well.

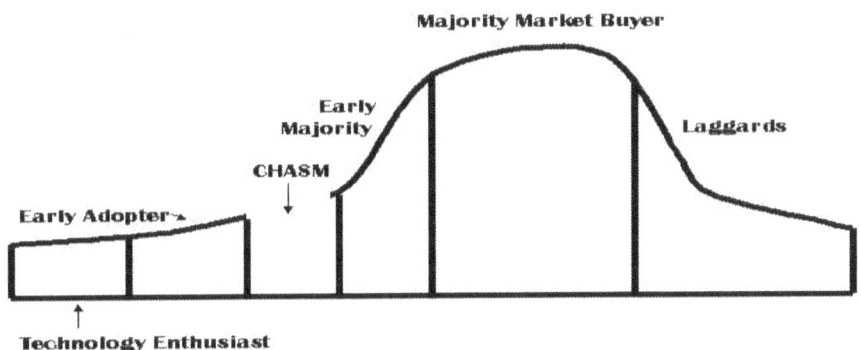

ConQuest's earliest and best reference account was Infonautics. Because Infonautics offered a service on Prodigy, and eventually the Internet, it was easy to point to and demonstrate the ConQuest search engine in live action. It was a third-party service and, therefore, gave us credibility. In fact, the target market of Infonautics was students in grades in K to 12. Hence, it was very simple to use. ConQuest had to pay for this reference account, however, through a substantial discount to Infonautics. But we recognized the value of this reference, especially for sales to other online services and publishers, and for that reason we were willing to offer the discount.

Not all customers are valuable reference accounts. Both ConQuest and Powerize had major customers in the pharmaceutical market. But due to the squeamishness of this market about trade secrets, neither company was ever allowed to state its customer list in the pharmaceutical market. Powerize had a major management consulting firm place its product in a technology showcase. That was nice, but it was not proof of usage. ConQuest had many government prototypes. These systems were usually experimental and not indicative of a mainstream customer. The best reference accounts are those that appear to be early majority and who are actually using your product in a needed business application.

Reference sits and beta customers are only valuable to you if they succeed. Your product must perform for them and they must use it. To get this to happen will take significant effort. First, you must talk to users and implementers within the customer organization and make certain your product is continuously improved until it meets their needs and delivers business benefits. Second, once the pilot is successful, you must aggressively work the organization on the inside to expose your product and get it adopted. Only then are you ready for a referral.

That said, with strategic partners, ready products, and reference accounts in hand, it's time to turn your attention to the organization of your company and the true penetration of your market.

Chapter 6

Designing the Culture

"Noble life demands a noble architecture for noble uses of noble men. Lack of culture means what it has always meant: ignoble civilization and therefore imminent downfall."
—*Frank Lloyd Wright*

According to the *American Heritage Dictionary*, the definition of culture, as it applies to a company or venture, is "the predominating attitudes and behavior that characterize the functioning of a group or organization." One of the most influencing forces in a professional organization is its culture. The culture of a company can be chosen and shaped by the individuals managing the company. If designed carefully, organizational culture can drive and motivate everyone from senior level personnel to part-time workers. It would stand to reason that the opposite is true too. If not designed carefully, the culture could define itself and lead your company to sub-optimal performance. To illustrate, this chapter will discuss the impact of management on organizational culture.

Defining Your Culture

Define your culture or your culture will define you. That is a very profound statement. It requires entrepreneurs to perform a function that they forget to do, don't know how to do, or simply choose not to do.

Culture consists of the shared beliefs, work protocols, peer expectations, value system, and guiding principles held by you and your entire staff. Defining your culture begins with the development of your vision, but your culture can be influenced by many other factors as well. Consider the following:

- Your work habits and value system will be keenly observed by many of your peers and subordinates, whether it is conscious or subconscious. Culture begins with you. Every day!
- The people you hire, especially the top leaders and early players, will have a similar but somewhat diminished influence upon the company. Screen them for their values as well as for their skills. The hiring habits of the company will also affect the behavior of your employees (i.e. giving preferential treatment to old friends is a bad idea).
- The work hours and the dress you keep—and allow others to keep—may become permanently ingrained.
- The degree to which you value and use employee opinions, the way you compensate your employees for their suggestions, the way you grant titles, and the overall value and appreciation you show to your staff drastically affects the culture of your company.
- The balance between engineers and marketers, and how you choose to manage both, matters. For example, if the input of sales people is quickly incorporated in your product, but the suggestion of an engineer is viewed as an unwarranted feature, a cultural backlash will occur.
- Your vision and mission statement, your horizon, and its explanation and buy-in obviously affect the culture of your company in a dramatic way.

- Your tolerance for missed deadlines, working hours, and the holidays, vacations, and benefits you provide all speak hidden messages. Watch out for expending too much generosity here because it sends the message that the company has more than adequate funds and there is no intense need to move fast. Once established by your employees, this misconception is a tough one to overwrite. Get a counselor on this if need be. A careful balance is needed.
- How much freedom and decision-making authority do you grant? It is important to treat people professionally, but you don't want to give them too much latitude. Your staff needs your leadership and guidance, even if both are occasionally challenged.

Often in the business of business, we lose sight of how simple actions are shaping your venture. However, if you define the culture you want to create in advance, many elements can be controlled to shape that culture including the management team and managerial style you establish.

Building Your Management Team

The management team is one of the most important elements of a new venture. Every book on raising money will tell you that it is better to have a first-rate management team and a second-rate product rather than having a first-rate product and a second rate management team. The same books will tell you that in order to be funded you must have a complete or near complete management team. Such warnings often cause founders of new ventures to run out and grab people with cool looking resumes just to create an instant management team even though some of these people will not be part of the real operational team. Those that have not been carefully selected may prove to be unqualified or disruptive to business. It is best to use a common sense approach to building a management team. First, you need to carefully identify whom you need and when you need them, and then you need to conduct an objective and methodical search for these people.

It is best to use a common sense approach to building a management team. First, you need to carefully identify whom you need and when you need them, and then you need to conduct an objective and methodical search for these people.

The logical way to start building your team is to first consider your venture's founders, you and any others on your team. Initially, you will be in control of the venture and your early decisions about management will have a profound influence upon the culture of the company. One of the first questions you need to ask yourself as founder is if you should also be the CEO or the CTO. There are arguments favoring both sides. Sometimes the best solution is for the founder to be CEO only until the venture has become established. At this point, the founder should bring in professional management. But this solution is not necessarily the right one for every venture.

Ownership and management are clearly two distinct things and they should never be confused. They cannot always be completely separated, however, because the principal management usually participates in company ownership—as well they should. The kind of person that founds a company is usually different from the kind of person that can successfully run an established company. Even in cases where the founder does become the CEO, sooner or later he or she is usually replaced or demoted to Chairman of the Board. Perhaps the most visible examples of this scenario are Bill Gates and Larry Ellison, founders of Microsoft and Oracle, respectively. They both served as CEO after their companies went public until they realized that there was a better person for the job, at which time they both gracefully stepped aside and assumed positions as Chairman.

All too often, the founder wants to be CEO for egotistical reasons. The founder should be willing to make room for another CEO if and when the board of directors determines that their doing so would be in the best interest of the company. A founder CEO who does not hold this attitude can be a liability to the company and an obstacle in raising capital. These people often build a board of directors that does not challenge them as a CEO. Ironically, founder CEOs who are open to the possibility of a new CEO taking over often retain their position as CEO longer than those who aren't open to this idea.

One option for the founder CEO is that he can choose to surround himself with additional management support to compensate for his weaknesses. I used this technique in running both ConQuest and Powerize. At ConQuest, I recruited a chairman because of his extensive network. This venture was my first and because of that, I was not yet well connected. Once involved with Powerize, however, I had accumulated a wealth of contacts. But I knew from prior experience that I was a visionary, externally focused CEO. I needed an operational manager to take care of the day-to-day details and manage people more closely. I brought in a Chief Operating Officer (COO) precisely for that purpose.

Filling Key Positions or CXOs

Every venture is unique. Each has unique management requirements that are derived from the horizon, mission, and operational needs of the company. That said, there are various classes of management positions that are usually needed at various stages in a venture.

In this section, we will take a look at a few of the most typical positions and the common sense reasoning about when these positions might need to be filled. Previously, we discussed establishing your founding team. Your management team expands upon that team, adding additional skill sets required by your company at this point in its development.

CEO: One part visionary, one part salesman and one part manager and one part analyst. A venture must always have a Chief Executive Officer— if not an official CEO, then an "acting CEO." Perhaps you have founded a company with your partners and you want for all of you to be equal.

That's nice, but there must never be any doubt about who is in charge. Aside from serving as the head honcho, the CEO must also promote the company's horizon, vision, and mission to all stakeholders, including employees, customers, and investors. Selecting the CEO is a very fundamental decision. If you are part of a seed-stage company, perhaps one of the founders is still serving as the CEO. If you are at a later stage and want to hire professional management, use your investors and advisors to help you. The entire management team should interview the prospective CEO to determine how well he or she will fit into the company, as well as how qualified he or she is.

COO: A Chief Operating Officer typically serves as the right-hand man of the CEO. Usually, this person runs the internal and operational side of the company. The CEO may be more externally focused, spending his time raising money, forming strategic alliances, or taking the company public. Under these circumstances, the CEO does not have the time to properly manage the company. Not all companies need a COO. A very early stage company, in which the CEO is one of the founders and product development is still the primary activity, does not normally need a separate COO. Usually the COO is a person who is procedurally oriented, perhaps entrepreneurial but not always from the founding team. This type of manager most likely has the bulk of his or her experience in an established business setting, ideally that of a business that has gone through a period of intense growth.

CTO: Part engineer/part businessman. CTOs that are 100 percent engineers don't work! We have already stated the necessity of having a CTO aboard from the very start in a high-tech company. An exception to this rule could be a non-technical company, perhaps one that has defined its horizon around a business process revolution that is not heavily dependent upon technology. However, engineers need leadership. The CTO must be able to earn the respect of the staff, based upon his skills and technical know-how. This should happen automatically if your CTO has the required expertise. Engineers are very perceptive and quick to assess if management understands the technology they are developing. Their respect goes to those who are in the know.

> **Engineers are very perceptive and quick to assess if management understands the technology they are developing. Their respect goes to those who are in the know.**

CFO: What exactly is a CFO? And when do you really need one? An accountant or controller may just as well serve your financial management needs in the beginning. One common mistake is giving a good controller the title of CFO. This is a major headache as the company grows. For most companies, it's not necessary to fill this position until you are nearing your public offering when SEC filings, Wall Street analysts, and larger administrative staffs are required. A Chief Financial Officer raises money; devises the financial strategy of the company; deals with investors, Wall Street, and the SEC; and has an administrative staff reporting to him or her. Sometimes your CFO can be an outsourced function provided by your venture capitalist. Another way to provide for this position is to have a person with a broad skill set serve your organization. When I started Powerize, I began the company with an experienced CFO who was also our controller, contracts specialist, HR manager, entrepreneur, and operational manager. He was part of the principal management team from the start because of his breadth of skills and entrepreneurial flair.

VP Sales and Marketing: Clearly, sales and marketing are not the same thing and do not involve the same people in any established business. They are lumped together to make a point. Many start-ups hire one person to fill both positions, and that person more than likely focuses on business development. Usually the VP of Sales is not part of the founding team, but the VP of Marketing is. Major headaches are in store if you give someone this combined title too early. Marketing serves a different function than sales. The role of marketing tends to be more essential to the company's definition, since it governs product positioning and management. These functions typically require attention earlier in a company's development than the later marketing functions of press relations and lead generation. The VP of Sales generally comes along once the product is finished, or is near finished, and the first few reference accounts have validated that the product will sell. Bringing in a VP of Sales or a sales force before this is a risky idea. At most, one good sales person can be hired early to help with filtering reference accounts and defining the sales program.

VP Business Development: Business development is yet another position found in most high-tech companies. Generally the VP Business Development serves to generate channels, revenue, and strategic alliances in areas that concern company issues other than those associated with released, off-the-shelf products. The duties of the VP Business Development may include technology licensing and joint ventures.

Another point that needs to be made concerning company positions is that the title "Vice-President" should not be used too liberally. The mere title grants signature authority. Even if the VP is not a designated officer, outside parties have no way of knowing that and they may assume, on the basis of title, that the VP has signature authority. For this reason, when a VP signs an agreement, it can be held as binding on the company. Banks are notorious for making a huge number of their employees VPs. However, this practice should be avoided in high-tech companies to avoid unnecessary complications that could divert your time and resources from more important matters. Title promotions in lieu of salary increases are a huge mistake. Look for people who don't need titles to fuel their egos.

Advisors and Board Members: Advisors have already been discussed at length in Chapter 3. Advisors are useful whenever they serve to cover a gap in your management team's skills, knowledge, or contacts. Appointing an advisor as a director to the corporation, however, should be done sparingly. Directors represent the shareholders and therefore must be elected by the shareholders. Your largest investors carry a large percentage of the votes and are usually represented on the board. But an outside advisor, invited in merely for his contacts, need not be on the board unless it will benefit the company in such ways as easy access to capital.

Technical Staff: Usually, your key technical staff members are aboard before many members of the management team. This circumstance can sometimes present team integration difficulties that could lead to turnover issues. This problem can be exacerbated if your technical staff does not provide good documentation. When they leave, they take the product with them by default. Mid-level technical employees who joined the company early may observe the hiring of senior managers who receive more ownership and equity than they did. Expectations must be managed to allow for this occurrence. As most people would agree, selection of your technical staff is very important to the success of your company. Ability to attract engineers will be essential to both your company and your investors. One or two technical people should be part of the founding team then you should staff up as required by your product development schedule. Bringing in too many technical personnel at once may negatively affect team building and group dynamics. People naturally form working relationships and establish a pecking order to avoid pandemonium and political battles for leadership roles. It is also important that your technical staff be recognized as a valuable part of the company. If you allow sales force to dominate management's attention, driven by the importance of revenue generation, you could inadvertently devalue the work of your engineers, who are just as important to your operations.

> **Selection of your technical staff is very important to the success of your company. Ability to attract engineers will be essential to both your company and your investors.**

Support Staff: Your support staff includes receptionists, executive assistants, and other non-managerial positions. Of course, the support staff should be paid the full market value. But an added bonus would be to grant these staff members a modest number of stock options. You will surely earn back your investment by ensuring that they feel part of the team. If there is an intentional or unintentional social scale, the company could develop a morale problem. Despite the fact that certain positions are generally easier to fill, any turnover costs time and money so it's important to treat all members of your staff fairly.

In closing this section, the following are a few general guidelines that are useful as you build your team, regardless of the position.

- Be careful about hiring friends, family, or spouses. You may not have the objectivity to accurately assess capabilities. If the hire ends up being a bad choice, you will have a messy situation on your hands, especially if they own stock.

- Do your own hiring. If at all possible, avoid headhunters. Many of these agencies charge a fee that you cannot afford and you may be stuck with a pool of job seekers that are less than stellar. Often the best recruits are already gainfully employed and need to be lured out by the excitement of your vision. Only you can do that effectively.

- Carefully perform a background check on your prospects. Call former employers and references. Find out if they have been let go in the past, filed for bankruptcy, or if they have sued any former employers. While former employers are only supposed to verify employment and title, you can often gather more information by asking open-ended questions. Ask questions such as, "What role is this person best suited for?" and try to read between the lines. Taking extra time during the hiring process can save you from making costly mistakes later. Criminal background checks will reveal substance abuse and psychological problems.

- Make your employment deals contingent on personal performance. Equity should not be granted outright, but instead based upon time or achievement milestones. A six-month trial period is often a good idea.

- Avoid the use of employment contracts whenever you can and hire at will. Demand a nondisclosure agreement. Also, demand that the person sign an intellectual property agreement insuring that whatever he or she develops related to your company's work will belong to the company. Sometimes you may want a non-compete agreement, but such contracts are often hard to enforce and can be difficult to obtain. If you must sign an employment agreement, be sure that you maintain the right to terminate for any reason and try to avoid severance pay as much as possible. Two to four weeks should be adequate in most cases.

- Weed out new employees that aren't good matches for your company. Non-performers and people who do not believe in your vision have no business being a part of a new venture. It only takes one disruptive person to defocus the company's efforts. And it only takes one non-performer to demoralize the rest of the staff. You will be judged harshly by the rest of your staff and your investors if you are reluctant and indecisive about firing people. There isn't room for a "one last chance" or to take a "let's make everybody happy" attitude. However, never let someone leave your company in a rage. Always terminate employment with a calm, cool, and collected demeanor. Base it upon the employee's poor performance or lack of allegiance to the company's mission.

- The importance of outstanding performance must be emphasized, but it must be done tactfully or you will appear to be a tyrant. Some major software companies have built excellent sales forces by letting go the sales people that performed in the bottom 10 percent of earnings each year, even if they beat their quota. This, however, may have morale drawbacks and a lower threshold might be selected.

- Remember as fact that as the company grows, people will leave and they will outgrow their roles.

On Motivation and Management

We have already discussed the topic of motivation, but we were mainly focusing on the motivation that arises from the division of company ownership. The motivation you need to inspire now is the desire to work hard, follow the horizon, be excited about it, and really execute the mission together as a team. This motivation always begins with an artful sharing of the vision. Here, the challenge is to achieve a balance between the original vision of the founders and the vision of the company shared by your entire team. Your staff needs to feel as if the company is their own.

Singularity of Vision

The horizon and the vision it brings to mind is one of the most compelling forces to attract others to be a part of your company. The vision must inspire the belief that it will change the world in a worthy way. Everyone must believe in the same vision. Achieving a singularity of vision should be your first managerial goal.

Once singularity of vision is achieved, it will have an accelerating effect on revenue.

How do you accomplish a singularity of vision? It begins with the founders who sell their vision, but it must continue with everyone that participates in the process of defining and refining the vision. Karl Albrecht, in *The Northbound Train*, provides one of the best-written sources on how to establish singularity of vision throughout an entire organization. The book guides you through the process of developing a vision and mission statement and getting everyone on board. Peter Senge, in *The Fifth Discipline*, also provides a well-written chapter on obtaining a shared vision. His process advocates defining a company's vision based upon a model of a learning organization—a company that learns from its experiences in the market. A learning organization is important to creating singularity of vision because it gives the team a common grounding of experience from which to work.

Singularity of vision has the power to guide an organization. Management and key staff members are given authority to execute their jobs in accordance with the vision. This system can work well if it is managed well. At ConQuest, after some turnover in the management ranks and several meetings coordinated by a professional team builder, singularity of vision was achieved. Upon reaching a shared vision, the company's sales tripled in less than six months.

Powerize underwent a period during which the vision of the company became unfocused when we tried to market too many product lines. It took a year of work to refocus the company. Once the refocusing occurred, revenue grew from $300,000 per quarter to $1.4 million per quarter in only twelve months. This accomplishment took several management teambuilding meetings in order to reach a consensus.

There are many important points to note here:

- Teambuilding, especially teambuilding mediated by a professional, is a very valuable function in a small enterprise.
- Those members of the team who do not subscribe to the company vision after the teambuilding is complete are disruptive to the company's mission and must be asked to leave.
- Once singularity of vision has been achieved, it will have an accelerating effect on revenue.
- Any major change, such as a merger or acquisition, will require more teambuilding and a need to refocus the company, which can take a year or more.

Many of you reading this book will have to live through it before you will truly buy into these theories. However, to the extent you are willing to take them on blind faith, you may obtain an immeasurable gain in productivity.

Recognizing the Work of Your Employees

Professional employees have a strong need to be recognized for their work efforts. A common belief in a start-up is that everyone hired in such a demanding environment should be a self-starter and a hard worker that does not need positive feedback. Although this belief is common, it is somewhat unfortunate because it can cause a loss of motivation. Professionals like a good salary, equity, and benefits, but usually they are more motivated by doing well in their field and being a part of something important. If you know and recognize this common motivational source, you can put it to work for you. Recognize your employees often! But make sure you give them honest feedback. Listen to their problems and their views. Invest your time in them through one-on-one discussions to build their sense of self as well as your organization.

Understanding the motivation of each individual team member is very important as well. Some people are under cash pressure at home and, to them, salary and bonus cash may be the most important short-term gain. For your company's sake, hopefully not too many of these people are present at start–up when you're cash hungry! Other employees may be intellectually motivated and have a desire to contribute to product development in a way that makes a difference. Sales people are often motivated by the short-term commission, not so much because they need the money, but more because they have a thirst for the power and independence that comes with the job. Founders are usually driven by a burning desire to change the world and make a lot of money in the process. However, be wary of those who are totally focused on monetary gain and do not truly have a passion for the company and its product or vision. Knowing the motivations of your employees gives clues as to how to recognize their work. The strongest compliments are those that pay personal tribute to your employees and also provide them with a strong hope of achieving personal objectives in the near future.

XYZ Management

Along with the Industrial Revolution came many managerial theories, including Douglas McGregor's Theory X and Theory Y assumptions about human nature as they are applied to the workplace. To summarize, Theory X assumes that people dislike work, seek to avoid responsibility, are not ambitious, and must be supervised closely. Theory Y assumes the opposite: that work is as natural as rest or play, that people do accept responsibility, can exercise self-control, and have the capacity to be innovative in their work. Theory X management is the type of management under which the boss tells everybody what they have to do and they go do it. Theory Y management allows for professional consensus to determine who does what; transforming a professional manager into a mere mediator.

A new venture needs to start out with management more like that described by Theory Y. However, once the company hits its first intense growth spurt, it may be necessary to make a temporary shift into Theory X.

Observing the behavior of high-tech ventures has led me to draw the conclusion that a new venture needs to start out with a managerial style more like that described by Theory Y. However, once the company hits its first intense growth spurt (or "tornado," as Geoffrey Moore would call it) it may be necessary to make a temporary shift into Theory X. There simply isn't time for consensus building when your company is on the verge of burn-through growth. Sometimes employees will be lost during this period, but such losses are almost always necessary in order to maintain control during peak times of business.

Now would be a good time to assess yourself in comparison to this entrepreneurial syndrome coined the "Admiral Halsey Syndrome," a nickname ascribed to me by a former employee during my first venture.

Fleet Admiral Halsey was famous for commanding destroyers during the World Wars. He was known for deciding what he wanted and going straight for it. The Admiral Halsey Syndrome often afflicts strongly motivated entrepreneurs and results in giving them the clarity of vision to see what they want and the power to achieve it. Oftentimes, such ambition blinds you to the skills and ideas of others on your team. This situation is a very common one among early stage entrepreneurs. They tend to think of themselves as "the company" and forget that they have a team. Sometimes, it seems as if they can get something done faster just by doing it alone. Usually they can, but it occasionally comes at the expense of angering their co-workers.

If you think you have the tendency to exhibit these traits, be careful. Some of your zeal is not only beneficial; it's absolutely necessary. But it is vitally important to use your team. Put them to work executing your vision and making decisions. If it's hard to relinquish control, take solace in the knowledge that you are commander-in-chief and you can overrule your employees when necessary. But at least listen to your team. The time you spend doing so will be returned to your venture in a multiplied effort on the part of your team.

One of the most important balances you must acquire is the balance between leading and managing. You absolutely must do both.

One way to begin leveraging your team is to make a practice of "managing by walking around." If you take the time to wander the halls and offices of your workplace, you will observe a lot, learn a lot, and interact more. You may hold five or six spontaneous meetings in the halls in just one day, and during each meeting, you might put some new forces to work executing something important. The people you ask to complete these tasks will feel good that you trust them to do so. It is absolutely necessary for the CEO to interact informally to help define the culture of the company.

The art of delegation is an important skill for you, the entrepreneur, and one that you must practice frequently. Use the resources you have. That's why you hired a staff and they will not stick around if they do not feel important. The CEO may, in fact, serve as an evaluator and a source of motivation more than a hands-on worker. Delegating to others is tough for many entrepreneurs who are naturally the hands-on type. A delicate balance is perhaps the right formula. One of the most important balances you must acquire is the balance between leading and managing your company. You absolutely must do both. A leader is greatly respected in a venture. However, a good manager is also necessary in order to maximize the output of the staff.

For additional reading on subtle management techniques and managing by walking around, refer to the article below, excerpted from *Meridians* magazine, which discusses how you can empower your team in indirect but motivating ways.

The techniques described in this chapter can be used as part of an overall strategy to design your culture. By applying them consistently toward your goals, the values of the company will become entrenched in the minds of your staff members. Remember, a conscious effort toward establishing your culture can be very valuable; a lack of it will lead to random cultural values that perhaps cannot easily be changed.

For Business Management, Surprising Insights
An entrepreneur discovers that the principles of nature used in acupuncture enhance his work in the business world.
By Edwin R. Addison
Summer 1998
Meridians magazine

I have always tended to be task-oriented in my work as a computer entrepreneur and CEO of a software firm. Goals drive the firm, and these goals get translated into specific tasks for individuals. They involve deadlines, sales quotas, expense limits, code creation and marketing events—all pursued with what an outsider might think is superhuman intensity. Many may not understand that a software company such as ours is driven by a compelling collective vision—the opportunity to create what never existed before. It is a team effort. Frenzy and what may seem like futility are part of the process. Recently, though, I've been surprised to learn effective new ways to handle challenges in a business on the edge of creation.

My new learning began in a two-week intensive called SOPHIA (School of Philosophy and Healing in Action), which I took at the Tai Sophia Institute. I enrolled in the course for the sake of my wife. She was beginning Tai Sophia Institute's master of acupuncture degree program, and I was interested in her career and wanted to support her. After all, I had been focused intensely on my own career over the years, and here was a chance to show that I cared about hers too. What I didn't anticipate (I was ignorant of the course content when I enrolled) was how much I would benefit in other ways.

SOPHIA teaches a "practitioner to life" concept, the idea that each of us can use knowledge about natural cycles and other relationships within nature—principles that underlie acupuncture—and apply them to all areas of life. In this way we can become "practitioners" to family life, to our relationships, organizations, and communities.

Creating by declaration

In one of the first SOPHIA sessions, our instructor marked a dot on a blank white board. That dot, the instructor pointed out, defined itself while also defining everything else, as "not it." This simple exercise called my attention to how we plan and create a business. Once we make a decision or a declaration, a vision begins to emerge out of nothingness—when we declare we are creating a software business, for example, we're obviously excluding a taco stand or a furniture store. Then, with each new decision and declaration, we further define our creation.

The power of language is used daily in business to define and create. Now I am more aware of this power and can use it more deliberately and with greater effectiveness. For example, when closing a sale, I'm careful to make clear declarations about every aspect of the arrangement so there are no gaps in understanding between the parties. Often I've seen sales reps lose a closing because they failed to define a position, sometimes introducing new issues too late in the negotiation (as when they tell a customer who has already agreed on a price about an alternate pricing scheme). They provoke uncertainty and lose the power created through thoughtful declaration.

Consciously cooperating with nature's creative cycle

SOPHIA introduced me to the creative cycle of the five elements— nature's wheel that turns from birth to growth, through maturity, harvest, and letting go, and then returns to a period of rest and renewal before beginning again. We know this cycle best as the yearly round of seasons. Yet the cycle shows up in every phase of life. Sometimes it takes only a few minutes to circle around, sometimes many years. After learning about the five elements, I came to see my first software company as having run the course of the seasons: The company began with a desire and a lot of uncertainty. For more than a year after I got the idea, I was afraid to leave my "secure" job and take the plunge (Winter). Once I had secured a modicum of funding and a talented business partner, we began creating a prototype and planning the business, step by step (Spring). Next, we fervently went about the task of building a product and finding customers. After we established ourselves (Summer), we became more valuable and sold out to a larger public company—a kind of "harvest" event for the team (Late Summer). I had a brief period of enjoying the fruits of all that effort and not working so hard (Autumn). After my obligations with the parent company were finished, I returned to the unknowing (Winter) and then began the cycle over again by forming a new company.

I also saw the creative cycle at work in other areas of our business—as when we identified a potential customer and went through the steps of contacting, educating, establishing a relationship, and completing the arrangement. Sometimes the creative cycle got "stuck" in one of its phases. In SOPHIA we learned ways to move the process along, just as acupuncture students learn to move stuck chi within an individual. For example, when a potential client resists hearing about what our company can offer him (Spring phase), we can make sure that he knows we understand the accomplishments and potential of his company. When he sees that he is dealing with people who appreciate the value of what he does, he becomes more open to working with us. (We learned in SOPHIA that one way to "treat" a blockage in the Spring phase of the cycle is to give acknowledgment and sincere respect.)

Becoming an observer

In SOPHIA I've learned to become an observer. I used to interpret communications from employees, customers and stockholders in a literal way. Now, increasingly, I go into "observer" mode, and I've discovered that the phenomena of business communications include much more than the words. To illustrate, when I asked our director of marketing why a certain item was missing from our web site, she told me, "My boss edited the text at the last minute." Once, I might have taken her reply at face value, but now my "observer" noticed that she spoke with frustration, even bitterness. When I probed for more information, I discovered that our company suffered from the "too many cooks in the kitchen" syndrome. Out of that discovery came improved lines of communication through which everyone could contribute ideas without disrupting the final work.

Restoring what's missing to a staff meeting

Last fall our staff was at a particularly intense place. With a major trade show and product launch just six weeks away, our weekly meetings had degenerated into statements about what hadn't been done and what actions we would take. Our schedules were severely overloaded, and the atmosphere was stressed and generally tense.

I decided to try out some of things I was learning in SOPHIA in one of our staff meetings. "We are going to run the staff meeting a little differently this week," I told the group. This got everyone's attention and they became unusually quiet. I then passed around a stack of my business cards, asked everyone to take one, write his or her name on the back, and return it to me. They complied and now were very curious about what I was going to do next. I shuffled the deck, then asked each person to take a card and note the name written on the back. They were not allowed to take their own name or the name of the person they worked with most closely. I asked them not to tell anyone the name they got.

Then I laid out the ground rules for the day's meeting. I began by stating that we all had been working under great stress trying to complete the "to do" list, and we had not taken time to notice what we had *accomplished*. So today, I said, instead of just each person reporting the status of his or her work and what needed to be done, we would go around the room several times. The first time, we would state only what we had accomplished in the last two weeks, without identifying what wasn't done or making apologies. After each person had talked, I remarked on the phenomenal amount of work we had accomplished. You could feel a lightness in the room—the tension had evaporated. This was a form of harvest, of taking in what had been done (Late Summer).

I then asked that we go around the group again. This time each employee was to pay a tribute to the person whose name they had received on the business card, acknowledging the contribution that this person made to the company. (In terms of Chinese medicine, this honoring of each contributor was a "Metal" or Autumn event).

Again we went around the room, this time reporting the current status of our projects without yielding to the temptation to jump in with solutions to any problems. We simply sat with the state of development just as it was, whether good, bad, or indifferent—a "Water" event (Winter).

Our last task was to create the action items necessary to move us forward—a "Wood" event (Spring). Then we concluded the meeting and proceeded to do the work that would move us to the next phase ("Fire"/Summer, the phase of maturity).

What a difference that meeting made! It eliminated tension, brought us close, and energized us as a team. So often in everyday business life we go straight from harvest to the growth of Spring. I've heard that in terms of Chinese medicine a short Autumn (a lack of acknowledgment) is cause for a blustery Spring—one reason, perhaps, that our workplaces are so fraught with emotional difficulty.

A new view of work

Occasionally, just to keep tuned in, I return to Tai Sophia Institute's SOPHIA class as a visitor. In this way I remain connected to my wife's career and, oh yes, each time I pick up something that influences my work. Students and instructors sometimes ask me if I'm planning to join the acupuncture degree program. I don't see that happening, but I do find ways to be a "practitioner to life." And viewing the business world through acupuncture's five-element lens helps me insure that no vital stages are missed in my work.

Chapter 7

Penetrating the Market

"I find that the harder I work, the more luck I seem to have."
—Thomas Jefferson

Penetrating the market is perhaps the most important task your venture will undertake. Often, it is one of the most daunting jobs for the first-time entrepreneur and its importance is sometimes underestimated. This chapter offers some practical advice on what it takes to penetrate new markets and guerrilla tactics for emerging as a known entity.

How Do We Get on the Map?

As an unknown in your business community, how do you become known? There are many ways to establish yourself as a known entity and usually no single way will do it. First and foremost, you have to become present in places where people expect to see vendors in your field. This includes being written about by the press, being visible with a few high profile customers, and earning the respect of technologists in your field. Achieving these things requires guerrilla work that includes seeking out opportunities and making careful decisions about the allocation of marketing resources.

How do you get on the map? This is the question that Internet e-commerce site Half.com was thinking about before its launch. They found the answer in a little town called Half Way, Oregon that agreed to change its name to Half.com. The ploy received a tremendous amount of worldwide press coverage that put Half.com on the map—literally and figuratively.

The Web site Half.com was an e-commerce site that aggregated liquidators and guaranteed to sell merchandise at no more than half the retail cost. The company's business model was positioned about halfway between Amazon.com and e-Bay. About twelve months after it was founded, Half.com was bought by e-Bay for more than $300 million in stock.

Not everyone can establish such instantaneous press coverage. But a step in the right direction is to place no boundaries on your ideas to gain notoriety. New ventures share common problems: no established brand, limited capital, and anonymity in their market sectors. To become established and make a powerful and sustainable market entry, guerilla tactics are needed. These smart and unconventional methods will begin to establish your presence. A few examples of some tactics you can apply include:
- Launching a thorough publicity campaign or creating a media event to get free press coverage
- Landing reference accounts with highly visible, respected players
- Finding inexpensive ways to expose the company to professionals who work in the targeted market sector
- Obtaining speaking and panel opportunities at trade shows
- Visiting industry analysts and getting covered by them

Lessons Learned by Dot-Bombs

Now that the Internet tidal wave has peaked, a few good dot-coms have mastered the Internet market, but many more are struggling to survive. Before your launch, let's learn from some of the misguided business principles that emerged during the onslaught of the Internet and see how the rules have changed since then.

Nothing can teach us more about how *not* to penetrate the market than the mass casualties of the dot-com era. Excess was the name of the game, funded by an irrational capital market. Common wisdom was to spend millions of dollars on brand identity to achieve the first mover advantage and to attract as much Internet traffic as possible. The common philosophy was to ignore revenue. The belief was that if you controlled traffic, you would eventually get the revenue. While the theory seemed plausible, it was unproven. The Internet and how it would be used by the mainstream was unknown. In time we learned that most Web surfers are disloyal and want things for free. They rarely click banner advertisements. As a result the Internet advertising market collapsed in late 2000. The only winners during this period were New York ad agencies. And so it was back to basics. To be taken seriously businesses had to make money.

Nothing can teach us more about how not to penetrate the market than the mass casualties of the dot-com era. Excess was the name of the game, funded by an irrational capital market.

The Internet is fertile ground for many innovative ventures. But one must go in with a solid business plan that includes proper exit strategies and timing. Black magic, common wisdom, and the desire to be part of the excitement are no substitute for a proven, working business model. The proof of any good business is a sustainable and ultimately profitable revenue stream. A company has no business going public without it. Those that go public early pay the price of a collapsing stock valuation. The "recession" of 2001 is the price we all paid for this time of excess.

Tony Perkins in *The Internet Bubble* was among the first to clearly predict the fall of Internet stocks in April 2000. Many now put some of the blame on the Silicon Valley venture capitalists and pundits for the inflated Internet valuation. After all, they made quotes such as saying that the Internet was "the largest legal creation of wealth in the history of mankind."

Enter the Netscape IPO of 1995 and a few others like it. The company went public when it had no business doing so. It took off wildly because of hype from venture capitalists, investment bankers, and day traders. The stock was heavily oversold, to the benefit of a few investors who were in before the IPO, just as it was with many other Internet IPOs. It guaranteed a same-day sale of stock for a higher price based on after market commitments from others.

Netscape created a capital market by exploiting the keiretsu concept. Members of the keiretsu were asked to buy from each other in a circular fashion (i.e. A buys from B, who buys from C, who buys from A, etc.) so that everyone's revenue is higher. Who pays the price when the bottom falls out of the market and there is no real capital? The consumer. In this case the venture capitalists did too because they never saw payoff. Now, everyone has learned and recovered. Hopefully.

The dot-com era closed in stages. First, in mid-1999 there were the first signs of broken IPOs (initial public offerings where the price drops on the opening day). The window started closing on new IPO opportunities by August 1999. Then private capital became more difficult to attain. In the spring of 2000 when Microsoft missed its earnings expectations, the Nasdaq got clobbered, followed by a three-month explosion of the dot-com bubble. Some stocks dropped in value by more than 90 percent. By September 2000, the stock market began to hurt and by summer 2001, fortunes had been lost. This, unfortunately, was part of the needed New Economy adjustment period.

As the bubble was bursting, it was interesting to watch some of the frustrations in the new start-up ranks. I listened to a question and answer session at a venture capital conference in 2000 where an entrepreneur raised his hand and asked a panel of venture capitalists why he couldn't get his company funded. His company was boxershorts.com and he was the first to sell boxer shorts on the Web. He didn't understand that his niche was extraordinarily narrow, the traditional retailers would blow him away, and the venture capitalists did not stand a chance at making a profit on his venture. Another company wanted to put personal bookmarks on the Web instead of the person's desktop. Nobody was interested for the same reason. The niche was too narrow, there was no real value, and companies with a real business like Yahoo would blow them out of business.

The lessons from dot-bombs are plentiful. So that you don't repeat the mistakes of the past, the chart below is a tongue-in-cheek list of the top ten beliefs of Internet companies in and around 1999. See if you can identify the business lesson that each belief teaches. As you read each, keep in mind the concepts that have been discussed throughout this book.

Dot-Com Top Ten Business Beliefs of 1999
10. If you build it they will come! Traffic on the Web is growing exponentially and by the laws of mathematical averages visitors will soon surf in. All you need are good links, banner ads, and a couple radio commercials.
9. The rules of business valuation have changed almost overnight. Things like marketing demographics and access to a customer base that are traded for advertising dollars are now worth more than things that cost money. The value of your business is based on eyeballs, not revenue and profits. This is because if you control eyeballs (visitors to your Web site), you can keep them and monetize them.
8. Internet advertising is the way of the future. This is because banner ads and click-through rates will just keep growing as usage of the Web grows exponentially. Anybody who decides to be the first one to give something away for free (such as content or products) is a real winner because they were the first to do it.
7. You must spend millions with a top-flight New York ad agency to create a brand name and then you must hire a PR agency to establish your brand and attract lots of eyeballs. Every dollar you give to one of these agencies will turn into hundreds of dollars in valuation. It's an instant multiplier. Quite simply—you just have to spend the dollars and you win.

6. Working your way to the top is too slow and unwise. Companies must be built fast. You must be venture-funded with at least $10 million to achieve the first mover advantage or else you might as well not even be in business.

5. The Internet works in warp speed. Product development cycles have shrunk to days. Everything must be done in Internet time and if you can't adjust then you'll go out of business.

4. If you patent a business model, your valuation will instantly soar—just like Priceline.com. And even though the business model is unproven, you don't need technology anymore, because the business model will drive sales.

3. If your name ends with dot-com you can go public at anytime—even before the company is officially founded—because public venture capital is "in" and the stockholders will believe you are displacing a brick and mortar company.

2. The old rules of stock trading are obsolete. You don't need revenue and nobody cares about profits if you are an Internet company that invests in marketing. Day traders provide liquidity, the lead underwriter will spin the stock, and momentum investors will always be there pushing the price up. Just check the stock bulletin boards because that's where inside information can be found.

1. You have to own Internet stocks because all brick and mortar companies are going out of business in the coming decade. We are passing from a real world to a virtual world. If you get caught without a piece of the action you'll be poor and everyone else will get rich. Price doesn't matter because there is a long boom out there and things are only going higher.

Not all dot-com ventures are destined to fail. But if you are going to develop a dot-com venture, you must apply practical business sense. Find value for your customers. Make real money. Use the principles in this book. Before you start your business is the time to flush fantasy and false pretense from your head. Instead, take positive steps to ensure that you launch your venture soundly. Have passion in your work—not just the almighty dollar—and take five to ten years to grow your business. Here are some suggestions on how to accomplish manageable growth and successfully penetrate your market.

Initial Market Penetration

The first order of business is to identify your beachhead market or the first market you are targeting. A young venture has limited resources. The worst thing you can do is chase every moving target just to get a buck. We already discussed the power of reference accounts. Hopefully, you are establishing reference accounts in this market.

> **A young venture has limited resources. The worst thing you can do is chase every moving target just to get a buck.**

Establishing a beachhead market has become the marketing mantra of Silicon Valley, due the popularity of Geoffrey Moore's *Crossing the Chasm*. You should adhere to this principle. Once the Internet was commercialized, this advice was forgotten in favor of ubiquity. The Web sites and dot-coms that were most successful focused on a narrow niche at first. A classic example is Amazon.com, which just sold books before branching out. You have to start somewhere but not everywhere. That dilutes your resources.

If you are market driven, your beachhead will have been defined by a vision that was focused on a market segment from the outset. If you are technology driven, you may need to apply some market analysis to your business. Choose a beachhead where you have a clear competitive advantage. Selling against competition is exhausting and it depletes precious resources. You are best served if your beachhead market has little competition. You can attack the more competitive market segments when you are stronger and have more momentum.

Your first customers should be limited to your defined beachhead market. Resist the temptation to sell outside this market. You may be tempted to try to expand your revenue base but it will dilute the focus of your resources and compromise the quality of your offering. I learned this lesson the hard way at ConQuest.

Our first sales group could not resist the temptation to shoot at any moving target. While our product was a search engine, it was sold as a CD-ROM search engine, a document management system, a Government Intelligence system, a litigation support software system, and a Lotus Notes manager—all in the first year it was on the market. The deals were closed, our engineers were frazzled, and the company was not dominant in any one area. It took a complete turnover of the original sales group to achieve the focus we needed, and upon doing so, the company's growth accelerated.

The value of reference accounts cannot be overstated. These accounts are ideally members of the beachhead market. Once established, you should pursue early customers with a vengeance. A lot of hard work, relationship building, and extending yourself and your company are needed. You are not just pursuing dollars at this point, but also market segment ownership. Landing the first few customers, doing a superb job and then spreading of the word can help you accomplish this.

In addition to your early selling effort, some branding work is in order. It is easy to spend megabucks trying to establish a brand and it is easy to fail in the process. A better approach for a seed-stage company is to use innovative tactics. This means a host of techniques designed to get the word out without giving all of your money away to New York ad agencies. As a simplistic example: press is free and advertising is expensive.

Press coverage is more credible than advertising because it comes from a third party. And it's not so hard to get. Why not focus on getting a few stories published on your company instead of buying a $20,000 full-page color ad in a magazine? Give speeches at conferences, visit with industry analysts, talk to your local reporters, announce news in press releases, provide and promote a first class Web page, hold press conferences, give seminars, leverage the visibility of your strategic partners, and network a lot. Do not buy advertisements, pay advertising and public relations agencies large retainers, or spend big bucks on image design yet. There is a time for that. But that's not until you have fully proven your business model and established a recurring business stream.

Market share is very, very important, but not at all costs. It must be achieved without going out of business!

Another strategy that was popular during the dot-com rush was to give away products for free. This seemed to be a takeoff on the old Boston Consulting Group philosophy of "market share at all cost." In the dot-com world, the strategy was to win eyeballs and grow ad revenue. While a few very well-funded, large risk bets can win this way, most such attempts fail miserably. The dot-com debacle put an end to that philosophy. Market share is very important, but not at all costs. It must be achieved without going out of business.

Now let's pause and assume that you have done everything we have discussed so far in this book. You have taken an idea, defined your horizon, sold your vision, recruited a team and a group of advisors, written a draft business plan, developed and tested a first product, defined a beachhead, obtained reference accounts and first customers, and established at least some of your management team. Wow, that's a lot of work! Now, and not before now, is the time to build a sales force.

Building the Early Sales Force

Leveraging the Horizon is not a substitute for a book on selling techniques or sales management. However, in the same anecdotal spirit as we have treated other areas of venture development, we will provide you with a few concepts based on real world experiences.

Deciding Your Sales Approach

Do you need feet on the street, channel managers, or telemarketers? Can you sell by direct mail or through the Web, and therefore need a direct marketing staff? Is your business going to be based on a few large deals that should be led by senior management? These are fundamental and important questions that your business plan should have addressed, but let's discuss a few of the basics here.

The nature of your audience, the way you will reach them, and the price point of your product will help you determine your sales and distribution strategy. Cost and competition will help you determine them. For example, high-end products are usually not sold by telemarketers. When was the last time you were eating dinner and someone called to ask if you would like to by a new Turbo Porsche 911 and you said, "Sure, where do I send the money?" Conversely, door-to-door salesmen generally do not sell low-priced products. When is the last time your doorbell rang and you were asked if you'd like to buy an upgrade of Microsoft Word?

The sales and distribution strategy you will form is not simple and may require that you perform a financial analysis of projected revenue, expense and market share before deciding on the best scenario for your business. Ultimately, the decision may not be based on analysis, but on what works most naturally.

Direct sales forces are very expensive. Often, high-tech ventures prefer to set up distribution channels and use resellers. While that saves on sales costs, you lose direct control of your customer. Some use a dual strategy combining direct and indirect sales. For instance, you may have a small direct sales force to land high-end, visible accounts and reference accounts. And then you may count on resellers to drive your volume and allow them to benefit from your marketing and reference accounts. More than likely, the sales and distribution strategy you will form is not simple and may require that you perform a financial analysis of projected revenue, expense, and market share before deciding on the best scenario for your business. Ultimately, the decision may not be based on analysis, but on what works most naturally in your field.

ConQuest underwent many changes in sales strategy before the best fit was found. The earliest sales force was brought in too soon. They were unable to close due to an immature product and lack of reference accounts. But this failure was also due to deploying a direct sales force and a price point that was too high for the market. A decision was made to shift to selling a search engine rather than a full document management system. This lowered the price point, warranting a shift to an indirect sales channel, putting several of our sales people out of work. Channel selling proved also to be difficult for ConQuest as the product was complex and resellers were slow to catch on. What ultimately worked best was using a small but talented direct sales force to sell the search engine and not the fully functioning document management system to select vertical markets. Two markets became very strong for ConQuest. These were publishers who were offering online services and government intelligence applications. But it took experimentation and the willingness to change when things didn't work to finally arrive at the right formula.

Picking Your Sales Staff

You are the best initial sales force. Use yourself in this role as much as you can and hire the sales force only *after* the product is refined and the reference accounts are in place. Then have your sales force proceed aggressively and methodically while you focus on the large, strategic opportunities.

Staffing for sales is a tough job. Once you have chosen your approach, the type of skills you need becomes clear. Choosing your VP of Sales is a very critical management team decision. This person will be in charge of driving revenue. He or she must be aligned with your vision of the company and the sales strategy that you have chosen. This does not mean that the VP of Sales does not get input on the approach to sales—quite the contrary. But picking the wrong VP of Sales can be a costly mistake and one that is highly disruptive to replace.

Many sales leaders have strong personalities and like a lot of control. That's what makes them good at sales. And that makes it even more important that this person be carefully integrated into your team. Too often, fast-paced ventures that are in a hurry to grow fill this position too quickly.

Picking the wrong VP of Sales can be a costly mistake and one that is highly disruptive to replace.

How about hiring the sales staff? Whether it is direct sales people, channel managers, or telemarketers, the manager they will report to should hire these people. When a person is hired, their loyalty goes with the person who hired them. In sales especially, it is vital that the person who will be the boss do the hiring. Certainly, some degree of consensus should be obtained for new hires, but the process should be led by the sales manager of the person to be hired. I have had several experiences where I have hired a sales rep, and then later hired their boss. This rarely works out. Sales is personality specific.

Hiring a sales team makes it necessary that compensation and commission plans be addressed. Immediate monetary awards motivate sales people. Commissions, more than equity, are what these people seek. It rewards them based on their own performance, which is also what you want. Should we use commissions to pay sales reps? Yes, if it has been established that your product can be sold. No, if it is too early in the game. But if that's the case, perhaps you should not be building a sales force.

Commission plans can be exceedingly time-consuming. If you are not experienced at designing a sales compensation plan, you should not do it yourself. Resist the temptation to apply your own formulas and get some professional advice. Otherwise you risk constantly changing your plan to solve unforeseen problems.

At ConQuest and Powerize both, redesigning commission plans when things went awry took endless hours of management time. This should be the job of the CFO with input from the VP of Sales and the CEO.

Forecasting Your Sales

"Zero to fifty million in five years" is the de facto forecast of early stage entrepreneurs who just don't know how to forecast their revenue yet. This is the proverbial hockey stick. Sales begin slowly and then suddenly soar. Unfortunately, entrepreneurs seem to think such a sales ploy will help them raise money. Instead it preys on the naiveté of the forecaster and serves to lower the company's valuation if money can be raised.

Entrepreneurs Hockey Stick

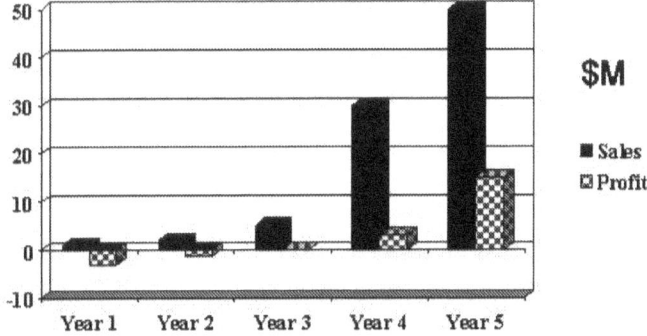

Sales forecasting is one of the most elusive and difficult tasks an early stage venture faces. Yet it can be as important as the life or death of your venture. How do you get your arms around a sales forecast when the product has no history, no market traction, and no historical numbers to project from yet? The answer is, you don't. The best you can do is to perform a scenario analysis. Build a model with reasonably conservative assumptions and see where it takes you. Then vary the parameters that represent the assumptions to see where the sensitivity points are. If you use even more conservative estimates for the most sensitive areas, you should get a projection you can beat. Use middle of the road assumptions to develop your best-case scenario and see where it lands. Present both cases to your investors and make sure you can explain all the assumptions in detail.

Have you allowed adequate delay for the decision-making time and budget cycle of your prospects? Have you allowed enough time for you to get the initial word out? Have you allowed for late collections and bad debt? Have you accounted for miscellaneous expenses including travel, expense reports, telephone bills, and incidentals? You can make a long list of questions like this and then try to answer them.

Should you use a business planning tool? Yes and no. As mentioned in Chapter 4, I am generally opposed to using business planning software for anything other than financial analysis. And even for financial analysis, which includes sales projections, the model should allow for reasonably detailed line item assumptions, or else you should not use it.

"Zero to fifty million in five years" is the de facto forecast of early stage entrepreneurs who just don't know how to forecast their revenue yet.

Our sales forecast was constantly moving at ConQuest. The reality was the business was not very easy to forecast. There were a certain number of large discrete sales that had unpredictable closing dates. These were usually shown in a spreadsheet as pending deals with a certain probability to close. While that is fine for a mental exercise, you cannot spend it. During the company's toughest time for cash flow, a lawsuit settlement with our landlord showed up in the sales forecast. Indeed it closed and we made payroll. But it was not revenue!

Businesses that have a recurring revenue model are easier to forecast than those that earn revenue upfront through discrete sales. This is because the recurring revenue stream is reliable. In the software industry, it used to be popular to grab all the revenue at once using the concept of a perpetual license. When a perpetual license was sold, the accountants allowed the revenue to be booked all at once. On the other hand, if a two-year license was sold, the revenue had to be recognized ratably over the two-year period on the books. This anomaly in software accounting led to much abuse in the industry. Technically speaking, perpetual license revenue should be recognized ratably over the average life of the software usage period. The same holds true for maintenance fees. It is important to become familiar with the rules of accounting and revenue recognition in your industry. Otherwise, a reliable forecast cannot be made. These rules are also useful in business planning.

Supporting the Sales Effort with Tactical Marketing

The following section highlights key marketing issues for the founding entrepreneur or early stage CEO. To supplement this reading, there are numerous books on high-technology marketing that are must-reads for anyone considering launching a venture. One excellent reference is William Davidow's *Marketing High Technology: An Insider's View*. Davidow gives a pragmatic overview of Silicon Valley-style product marketing, including sixteen principles for managing an effective marketing program. While the book is pre-Internet, it is a frank overview of marketing techniques you need to know.

Your Web Site

The tactical marketing effort should begin with your Web site. Your Web site is the first place people go to find out who you are. This is the place to display your horizon for the world to see. But you must also clearly state who you are today if your vision is too far on the horizon for prospects to clearly see. Sometimes there is a concern about raising the flag too soon and often ventures will operate in stealth mode until the product is nearing a market-ready condition. A Web site should be established by the time you sell your product, or sooner if you feel it will benefit your marketing effort.

Clearly, you want to put a lot of careful effort into your Web site design. While early stage companies are always cautioned to spend money wisely, this is one area besides legal and accounting services that I recommend you contract out. Professional designers do the best Web design. Resist the temptation to do it yourself. This is your image to the outside world and if you portray yourself in an amateur light, you will be viewed that way.

In your company's early days, there should not be large need to spend on collateral development. Your Web site is your collateral. You may provide white papers and other materials created through desktop publishing systems. However, until you are well onto your growth curve, printing thousands upon thousands of glossy flyers is usually unnecessary. Your sales department will think otherwise.

Activity in Professional Societies

Active participation in a professional society can be highly beneficial. The best professional societies to join are those that are heavily attended by your targeted customers. You will extend your network significantly and potentially acquire many speaking opportunities at meetings and events.

When I was CEO of ConQuest and Powerize, I spent a lot of time with the Information Industry Association. Now known as the Software and Information Industry Association (SIIA), this organization was previously focused on content and publishing. Publishers were target customers of ConQuest and suppliers to Powerize. By attending many meetings and participating in committees, I was able to meet executives of many prospects who eventually became customers. ConQuest was often prominently featured at meetings or representatives were invited to speak. In 1994, I was named "Entrepreneur of the Year" by this organization for the growth record and product innovations at ConQuest. This exposure led to more business. Our overall high level of activity was responsible for a significant portion of our business at ConQuest. Ultimately, it was extremely valuable in acquiring publisher relationships for Powerize.

Doing Press and Analyst Tours

"Influence the influencers" is a prime rule of good tactical marketing. It is important to get out there and meet the analysts in your field and find out where they think the field is headed. Expose them to your product and allow them to give you advice and direction. Then take some of that advice and give them credit for it. Eventually you will receive coverage in their reports for helping them with their mission. Do the same with the trade press. However, it is important to get analyst coverage first, because that is what the trade press will look for before they cover you. You will need to budget several weeks per year for these tours.

Young ventures love to go to trade shows. It is somehow proof that they are real. Trade shows can be of great value and can also be a tremendous waste of time.

In general, you should not do this yourself, but instead engage a good public relations (PR) firm. PR firms come in all sizes and budgets. If you're a young venture and cannot afford a top PR firm, you may start out with a smaller one that focuses on start-up companies.

In Powerize's early days, we used a firm that serviced high-tech companies among others. We received the royal treatment from these folks, perhaps even more than we sought. Our agent set up an analyst and media tour, making all the appointments and driving us from one appointment to the next. All we had to do was go along for the ride. Of course, we planned the presentation ahead of time. We did this in Boston, New York, San Francisco, and D.C. and obtained noticeable exposure at a cost of about $5,000 to $10,000 per month plus expenses for several months.

Trade Shows

Young ventures love to go to trade shows. It is somehow proof that they are real. Trade shows can be of great value and can also be a tremendous waste of time. There is an entire industry that thrives on people going to trade shows. The questions are which trade shows should you go to and why should you go? Should you attend or exhibit? There are different classes of trade shows and in practical reality, they serve different needs for young ventures. Consider each of these types:

- *Major trade shows offered in exhibition halls of major cities and drawing 10,000+ attendees.* These shows are expensive and are usually PR plays. Rarely are sales made at these shows, however. Watch out for "gotta be there mentality." The real winners in these shows are the media companies who produce them.
- *Industry trade shows that draw several hundred to a couple thousand people.* These shows are more focused but are still quite large. They may represent an opportunity for business development and meeting with other players in the industry.
- *Small niche workshops consisting of one or two hundred people.* These are often highly focused and a better forum for finding real customers. They are not a good forum for PR because very little of the press will attend them.

There may be other reasons to attend trade shows as well. Perhaps you have a product release and you want to use a specific show to instill a deadline at your company. In that case, the trade show is being used as a management tool. I have used this technique at both Powerize and ConQuest effectively. It raises no questions in the minds of your staff about arbitrary deadlines.

The important thing is that you always know *why* you are attending a specific show. This may help you decide to go for a small or a larger booth and whether to attend at all.

Using Advertising

How about advertising? I am generally opposed to both print and Web advertising as well as radio and TV for promoting high-technology ventures at seed stage. Many ventures could skip this type of marketing altogether. There are exceptions, and if you are extraordinarily well-funded (i.e. $50 million+) and need to build a brand, then the story changes. Sometimes it may pay to take an inexpensive ad in a local technology paper seeking beta sites or partners. This may be considered tacky for established ventures, but for zero-stage bootstrappers it is not.

ConQuest did just that. We advertised for beta sites in *Washington Technology* in its early days and found several beta sites and a couple of resellers as well. It also served to dredge up competition.

Winning Deals in a Competitive World

One of the best ways to beat your competition is not to have any. Of course, any entrepreneur who tells an investor that they have no competition may be immediately eliminated from consideration for demonstrating that he or she does not understand the market. Of course you have competition. But when the competition is not direct and in the form of substitutes, alternatives, and market entrants who haven't arrived yet, then you have the market lead on your turf.

The best way to achieve this desirable position is through proper business positioning, product market positioning, and business concept revolution. These measures will enable you to side-step your competition rather than getting right in their face. Your selection of an early market niche can also help here. When you have less competitive friction in your beachhead market, you can move faster and penetrate more deeply. Then later when the competition emerges, you will be more entrenched.

Of course, we do not always have this luxury. Competition can be good, even if it does take a toll on your pocketbook. Competition causes companies to become better. If you are in a beachhead market where there are head-to-head competitors, you will be under early pressure to prove that you have the best, most fully featured, well-funded, and mature product. Since you probably won't have all of these things, it will take a lot of personal selling and relationship building to overcome the disadvantage. It can be done, but it is not the easiest and least expensive way to go.

One of the best ways to beat your competition is not to have any.

Competitors often don't take too kindly to each other. ConQuest had a well-funded competitor, Verity, which offered a concept-based search engine. We competed directly on occasional bids. On one occasion in 1992, a sales rep from Verity called me in search of a job. I invited him in for an interview and we began working together for a number of years. A few days after I first hired him, I received a hand-delivered packet from Verity's lawyers. In it was a letter with a lot of threats but no substance and hinted that they would file suit if we acted on trade secrets. We got our lawyer to write a cordial but firm response, and we never heard from them again.

Hiring a sales rep or engineer from a competitor can be a good catch, but I would not recommend wasting a lot of time chasing such a deal. Wait for it to come to you. You have better things to do with your time.

When you are in direct competition for a large deal, winning almost needs to be approached similarly to the way a lawyer would try to win a court case. You have to learn every detail about the customer and the competitor. Then, you need to present your case to your prospect as if the prospect is the judge. The more time and effort you put into winning your case, the better your chance at success. A few war stories about ConQuest's early days best illustrate this.

ConQuest was innovative but was selling into an entrenched market of incumbents with lesser technology. We were able to unseat a major competitor in a multi-thousand "seat" deal by consistently delivering what the customer wanted. Not only did the search engine score well in competitive testing, but we were willing to develop various custom features to win the deal. At the time the competitor was ignoring this customer. When an incumbent is preoccupied like this, it can be a major selling opportunity. This particular deal made up a significant percentage of our revenue at the time and made a major difference in our ultimate exit strategy.

In another situation, a major newspaper publisher issued a request for proposal (RFP) for a multi-site information retrieval system for the archives of many newspapers. While most of the requirements in the RFP were directed at the text retrieval system, the RFP stated that the system must be procured from a major systems integrator with the text retrieval vendor as a subcontractor. It so happened that ConQuest was experienced in writing RFP responses and the norm for the industry was for text retrieval vendors to respond to smaller RFPs with a simple spec sheet and price table. ConQuest wrote a hundred-page response addressing all the requirements of the RFP. We provided this to any system integrator who wanted to work with us on a nonexclusive basis. Because we did all the proposal writing, there was limited bid expense for the integrators and more than half of them chose us. When the publisher did the competitive evaluation, we were the subcontractor on the top four teams. Our strategy worked. We won the battle and lost the war on this one, however, because the publisher's project was canceled by higher management due to a budget shift.

We did not make the right decision on every deal. Another major news publisher issued a similar RFP and we opted not to bid. We had limited information and we felt that the deal was rigged for an incumbent. We were wrong. One of our weaker competitors took the deal and subsequently won another half-dozen deals in the news publishing market sector using this as a reference account. We made a major blunder. By choosing not to bid, we lost several large deals.

Selling to Your Strengths

It is easy to get pulled into the fray of somebody else's game when competing for business. Remember to always sell to your strengths. Always go back to your horizon and tell the compelling story. This way you are playing on your terms and not someone else's.

As an example, ConQuest would always return to the search accuracy argument and tell the story of how the underlying semantic network was derived from linguistics. This gave us a compelling story and always called for extra consideration. This was our glitz.

Every company can have a network and a "keiretsu," whether or not Kleiner Perkins funds your business. Create it and use it!

It may not always be obvious where your strengths are. At ConQuest, we discovered that we had the fastest keyword search engine on the market by accident. ConQuest was not built to be a keyword search engine, but a natural language search engine. To test our technology, we had to do many searches for each user query. We had to conduct an index look-up for every word and every related word meaning and then statistically combine the results. This means we had to do about ten times more searching than any other search engine. That forced us to engineer our individual searches to be blazing fast. So by keeping our eyes on our horizon, we built a better keyword search engine, which is where the market was at the time. When we discovered that, we also sold our keyword search engine as a separately priced product and we gained a lot of new business in that manner.

The Keiretsu Effect

We have emphasized strategic partners and the need for a keiretsu emphatically. Assuming you've established both, it's time to leverage them to leverage *your* horizon.

Part of penetrating your market involves using your entire network as your virtual extended sales force. How do you do this? Make sure your partners' goals are aligned with yours. If they are reselling your product as part of theirs, their interests are aligned. If they need to roll out your product to their entire employee base over time, their interests are aligned. If they are project-driven and will use your product as part of a customer solution whenever it fits, their interests are only partially aligned with yours. In this case you cannot count on revenue or market penetration from them unless you are lucky and extremely persistent. You may have to support sales calls that never close.

This was the case with a partnership that ConQuest had with a large government contractor. One single license was sold to the contractor, and even then they tried to get it for free. ConQuest was asked to support and finance sales calls for this customer at our own expense. Most of these calls never closed. One day the partner decided to discontinue the product line that used the ConQuest search engine. Their interests were in using ConQuest to win service jobs. Only a tiny percentage of the revenue ever went to ConQuest.

Every company can have a network and a "keiretsu," whether or not Kleiner Perkins funds your business. Create it and use it!

What is a keiretsu? It is a powerful extended network. How do you get one and use it? Consider any and all of these sources:
- Your strategic partners—all of them
- Your largest customers—they may become resellers.
- Your investors—they may introduce you to customers.
- Your lawyers—they want to keep your business. They are good networking resources.

- Your suppliers—they will sell more of their product if they promote your product or use your product.
- Your customers' competitors—they may want to keep up with your customers. Go sell to them.
- Your service providers (lawyers, accountants, consultants, insurance providers, etc.)—they may become your customers.
- Your employees, who may be sources of referrals
- Your industry associations and shareholders, who may be customers or referral sources
- Other businesses in your vicinity that are sometimes the most overlooked prospects

Powerize.com was a business information service on the Internet. It aggregated information from fifty information sources, which included several thousand publishers. The information was sold on the Web through subscriptions and was offered for free courtesy of banner ads. Powerize had about twenty-five distributors—other Web sites and services that also provided information. To leverage this vast network of resources, Powerize promoted its service to the employees of its publisher suppliers and to the visitors of its affiliate Web sites through hyperlinks and online advertising. This enabled a rapid build-up of registered users from 10,000 to over 500,000 in less than twelve months.

Leveraging your network is not only key to penetrating the market, but it is vital to achieving a high growth rate once you are established. Strategic marketing should then be a regular business function. This leads us to the next subject. Once you have penetrated the market, the next logical step is growth. Achieving rapid growth is the subject of the next chapter.

Chapter 8

Funding the Venture

"Lack of money is no obstacle. Lack of an idea is an obstacle."
—Ken Hakuta

Seeking funding to build a venture is one of the most talked-about and misunderstood areas of interest among entrepreneurs. Many dream of landing a fistful of money but don't realize that raising money is extremely time-consuming and that more often than not the money goes to those who are already running a successful business. There are very few times like 1998 to 2000 when venture capital was easy to acquire at the seed stage. Seeking funding will consume substantial amounts of time. This chapter provides an overview of some of the steps you will need to take and some considerations you will need to make not only to attract venture capital, but to also get the right funding. Beyond VC, this chapter addresses all colors of money, including bootstrapping. Some preliminary thoughts to keep in mind regarding financing your venture:

- Not every company/entrepreneur should take venture capital.
- Funding the company might require a combination of strategies in this chapter.

- Timing is key.
- Taking outside money means a loss of control and new responsibilities.

Healthy Bootstrapping

What is bootstrapping? It is every possible means for your business to stay alive without a large infusion of capital. This is an art you must learn if you want to insure that you stay around when times get tough—notice I didn't say *if* times get tough. Your business will never fail but you might quit. What is important is to have a back-up plan for your back-up plan so that you can overcome challenge after challenge.

> **Nothing is better than a real sale! Obviously, make as many of these as you can.**

Bootstrapping takes many forms. These include everything from working for free and selling equity for labor to using consulting contracts for you and your employees to carry you through development. Don't forget about government contracts and small business support or artfully using "vendor financing" by paying a little bit late, using credit card loans, borrowing from Grandma, using your home equity line, getting a late payment from a supplier, giving a discount to a reseller, etc. Of course, nothing is better than a real sale! Obviously, make as many of these as you can. And as you bootstrap, it goes without saying to operate with integrity if you intend to establish any credibility. It is equally important not to let yourself get so upside down with debt that you cannot recover or raise capital. It is also important to set limits on the level of personal debt you can incur to finance your business.

By starting with healthy bootstrapping, you create good habits and discipline that will benefit your culture later. Healthy bootstrapping enables you to maintain positive cash flow without the death spiral of delayed payments, missed payrolls, and not being able to pay the rent to the point that employees and customers leave.

ConQuest was founded in 1990 and did not receive its first institutional investment until 1993. The first several years were managed through healthy bootstrapping and government funding. The text box below will give you a sense of how multiple sources of cash and cash equivalents were used not only to survive but to grow the organization to about thirty people during this period.

ConQuest Bootstrapping

The following outlines a dozen methods that ConQuest used to keep its business operating and staff growing during its early development years. It illustrates the diligence and persistence needed to build a venture through the formative stages.

1. **Founders Investment.** The two founders of ConQuest put $80,000 into the company bank account on the day they began full-time work

2. **Going Lean.** The first five employees did not take pay for the first year they worked. They received founder's equity instead.

3. **Minimizing Expenses.** Travel was conducted by car, not by plane, whenever possible. Inexpensive rent, finding services for barter, and avoiding extravagant benefits and fancy furniture were used to keep cost down.

4. **Small Business Innovation Research (SBIR) Funding.** ConQuest sought and won about eight SBIR contracts over the first several years. This was government funding used for product development.

5. **Hiring for Stock.** The first two dozen employees were offered the opportunity to give up salary in exchange for additional stock options. All of them took advantage of this, some more than others as they could afford.

---

6. **Friends and Family.** A private placement was raised from friends and family totaling $150,000 in the second year. These investors made a return of ten to one or more on their money in less than five years.

7. **Consulting and Teaching Income.** The early founders supplemented their income from outside sources to keep the draw on the company to a minimum.

8. **Maryland Industrial Partnership Grant.** The company won a grant from the state of Maryland to provide support to a university professor. The company paid 10 percent and the state paid 90 percent and the university work was focused on company product testing.

9. **Government Agency Service Contract.** The company won a contract from a government agency to evaluate technology. That contract provided cash, but also paved the way to a sale of our product to that agency.

10. **Maryland Challenge Investment.** The company received a near equity loan from the state of Maryland to support marketing of its new product and for job growth in Maryland.

11. **Reseller Discounts.** When the first product was released, the first several resellers were given deep discounts in trade for cash advances.

12. **Large Dollar Customers.** Early sales efforts were focused on corporate accounts that needed our technology for competitive advantage. We sought several six and seven figure license fees.

To be successful in making it through the start-up, an organization needs a tight-knit team. Everyone must pull in the same direction. It is ideal if there is a company-first attitude that is built into the culture to drive the company through lean times. Then when times do get tough, the company can meet as a group to discuss and solve cash-flow problems. At the start-up phase, keep no secrets and more than likely everyone will stick by the company, even when there is no money in the bank. You saw the opposite attitude during the Internet boom when there was a me-first attitude. This phenomenon was industry-wide and eventually the industry corrected for it.

It is ideal if there is a company-first attitude that is built into the culture to drive the company through lean times.

What about the downside of bootstrapping? For a high-potential venture, you cannot bootstrap all the way and reach your optimum market penetration. The ideal time to seek growth capital is after the following events have occurred:

1. Your basic team is in place.
2. Your product has been proven and or reached first release.
3. Your company has revenue, preferably several hundred thousand dollars.
4. You can make a credible projection showing that break-even is attainable on the first investment.

The world does not always cooperate and you may need cash before this point. Or you may be able to go alone for a longer period of time. There are some drawbacks to excessive bootstrapping, however. For example, your growth rate may be impeded by your reluctance to spend aggressively on marketing efforts. Or, you may pick the wrong people for the wrong reasons. For example, you may hire an officer just because the salary requirement is low rather than picking the best person for the job.

The key is to know when to throw the switch from bootstrapping to aggressive progress.

Obtaining Seed Funding

Seed funding is the first funding a venture receives before it has a product to sell or a source of revenue. It is the most difficult and expensive kind of money, but it is needed except in the most fortunate of circumstances when bootstrapping or revenue funds your growth. Seed funding is purely a conceptual sell. There are no financial statements yet. There is no product yet. You must communicate your passion for reaching the horizon, not just your drive to make money. You are selling your ability to make money for your investors based on things you haven't done yet.

What sources of seed funding should you consider? First and foremost, consider early adopter sales if you can close them. Revenue is the best kind of money above all others, bar none, but it often comes is small doses. That presents a real dilemma to the entrepreneur who has to decide how to spend his or her time—making money or building the company. Before a product is ready for sale, a company can consider consulting services, development services, government contracts, or pre-paid license. Or you may be able to find a corporate partner that will need you for a competitive advantage.

The most often used source of seed capital is the private placement. A private placement is typically an investment by an institution, friends and family, angel investors, or wealthy, accredited individuals with a $1 million net worth or $200,000 annual income. Your company usually sets the price and manages this type of funding with the documents drafted by your legal counsel. To properly do a private placement, a legally valid Private Placement Memorandum (PPM) must be prepared. Never try to do this without a lawyer. The SEC laws are very complex in this area. If you make a mistake early in your venture life, it may be difficult or impossible to raise money later. Powerize did a series of private placements during a time when the market was booming. The first placement was to friends and family, the second was through a boutique investment banking firm with wealthy clientele, and the third was to a small public company and its officers. As a result, we had two hundred shareholders, which was quite unwieldy. But we did have capital.

Beyond your own financial resources, friends and family may be the best sources of initial money simply because they know and trust you. But you may be able to get only a limited amount of funds this way and therefore have to look to other people. Getting money from other wealthy professional people that you don't know well is possible, but I recommend against that approach. You will end up with a stockholder following that could be trouble if you do not do well. Further, later stage venture capitalists dislike contending with a lot of outside shareholders. They generally want to see the ownership and motivation inside the corporation or closely held.

A good source is angel financing. It became popular during the dot-com days for any accredited investor to call themselves an "angel." This is not always the case. Accredited investors can sometimes be passive investors with extra money. An angel is an entrepreneur who has enjoyed previous success so he or she is in a position to help you in ways other than just money. In fact, sometimes an angel will be an advisor who does not put in cash. That may be beneficial to you as well if the angel investor can help you with strategy or networking. The right angel can add credibility to your management team. Equally true is that the wrong angel can make it difficult to raise a venture round later. It may bring up questions about your judgment, ability to manage, or both.

There are some venture funds that specialize in seed rounds, though not very many. These organizations may be helpful as well, provided there is a good link between the fund, its knowledge and experience, and your company. Keep in mind that soliciting venture money at this stage is very time-consuming and competitive and it is expensive in terms of equity you will need to give in exchange. As you are likely aware, the odds are stacked against you. Before heading down this path, make a good business judgment as to the likelihood of success and determine if it's the best fit with your planned funding rollout.

An "angel" is a cashed-out entrepreneur who is wealthy, knows your market, and may be investing to come along for the ride rather than to make a quick buck. Further, the right angel can add credibility to your management team.

Securing corporate partners may be a better route. Corporate partners that invest come along fully aware of potential pitfalls. But just like a private placement or a venture fund, it is important to pick the right corporate partner. All too often, entrepreneurs will chase any moving target with a dollar sign on it and then pay the price later for a bad selection. Be sure of your partners' intentions and all of the potential long-term fallout of this partnership. ConQuest secured its venture round from Motorola New Ventures in 1993. As mentioned previously, the reason Motorola invested in a search engine company was that it had a corporate investment in a new online service that needed the search engine. The online service failed. But both ConQuest and Motorola did well. ConQuest received much-needed funds and Motorola tripled its money on its investment in ConQuest.

There are numerous kinds of government support contracts that small businesses can seek. Most of this money either takes a long time to acquire or is highly competitive, but it may be worthwhile to pursue this source if you have the requisite talents. The Federal Government provides support to small businesses in the form of SBIR contracts. State and local governments often have loan programs, venture funds, or outright grants aimed at keeping companies within their state or jurisdiction. Small Business Association loans (SBA) are another source, but they are usually for established companies with profitability, not ventures. Securing government contracts from one or more of the federal research laboratories is another way to fund product development, provided you carefully negotiate for the intellectual property rights.

Obtaining seed funding is an acid test of your business. It will test you and give you practice at conveying your vision and message. If you cannot obtain some funds here, then how will you attract customers later? In essence, this phase tests you as a salesperson and your ability to sell your vision and product or service.

The availability of seed capital and the ease with which it can be obtained varies dramatically with the state of the economy. The best way to deal with the variable availability of money is to stay lean and learn to bootstrap so that you are viable when money becomes available. Bootstrapping comes naturally in times of downturn because people are willing to work for less or sometimes for nothing temporarily.

Regardless of the source of seed funds, you will need most of the following prerequisites to obtain funds. It is a good idea to prepare them in advance.

- A business plan
- A technical proposal or product spec
- A convincing presentation
- Good personal rapport with the funding source
- Proper legal and accounting counsel
- Professional reference/customer references

Seed money is precious. It should be spent sparingly. A good rule of thumb is that if an item is not directly in the path leading to revenue, don't use your hard-earned cash on it. Seed money is for out-of-pocket start-up expenses, proof of principle development, development of a first salable product or service, seeking early corporate partners, writing government proposals, and bringing aboard a critical but lean staff to start the business.

As precious as seed money is, it can also be a mistake to take money from the wrong funding partner. Not all money is the same. You need a funding partner who understands your business, who is patient, and who does not have a hidden agenda. It is ideal if the partner can put more money in when you need it. Getting the wrong investor can cause anything from an annoying distraction to an early demand for repayment to a time-consuming and expensive legal battle.

Powerize.com had such an experience with an investor. We received a several million dollar investment from a small company whose principals were as eager as we were for a quick IPO. When the window closed on dot-com IPOs before our filing was complete, we had to turn to the private capital markets for additional cash. Our investors were not happy. They began placing unreasonable terms on the payback of their funds. The capital markets were getting tighter. The investors had little interest in our business. They were being chided by their board and in hindsight were only interested in making a quick buck. We staved off a confrontation and ugly end to our differences when we merged with Hoover's Online. But a more careful selection of our funding partners would have saved everyone a lot of grief.

Seed money is precious. It should be spent very sparingly. A good rule of thumb is that if an item is not directly in the path leading to revenue, don't use your hard earned cash on it.

Choose your investors carefully. Do your due diligence and pick the ones that can help you in ways other than just money. Researching an investor is just as important as the research the investor performs on you. Look for money from patient sources. You are not just raising money, but acquiring a partner.

Another mistake young companies make is to spend seed money unwisely or lavishly and run out of money before there are other funding sources or before established revenue is in place. Usually when these mistakes are made, it is an indication that priorities are in the wrong place.

For example, it should go without saying that seed funding should not be used for:

- high salaries for founders, management or outside consultants;
- fancy offices, cars, parties, extravagant dinners, etc.;
- lawyer bills beyond a few hundred dollars for set-up; or
- big accounting audits.

Seed money is to prepare you to do real business. It should be used to complete your prototype, round out your initial team, get your beta sites, and establish initial revenue streams if possible. Once you have accomplished these basic steps you are ready for what is often called start-up funding or early-stage financing. This next step is at the time of initial revenue, but before the high-growth stage that usually just precedes an IPO. Many ventures will seek venture capital for this stage of financing. The venture capital campaign is discussed in the next section. Alternative sources of capital are discussed in the following section.

Seeking Venture Capital

Most entrepreneurial ventures never receive venture capital. At any given point in time the figure may be less than 2 percent or so that are venture funded. However, most ventures that eventually go public were venture funded. This figure may be closer to 67 percent. Some notable companies never received venture capital. Oracle and Microsoft are two of them. In fact, most start-ups should not get venture capital financing.

Qualifying for Venture Capital

Venture capital is for a particular kind of venture. Usually it is one that can return ten times on the dollar for the venture capitalist in three to seven years. That means a strong foothold on a large market. Sometimes the venture has great technology but the market is too small for a VC play. Other times the market is large, but entrenched competition makes the

VC play too risky. Some ventures have the potential and there is no other way to get there.

Consider US Internetworking (USi), one of the earliest Application Software Providers (ASP) on the Web, a capital-intense business. It "rents" software on the Web to client companies. Typically, USi must purchase high-end software up front, then make it available to its clients via their own machines and bandwidth. USi made money based on software rental and service, but its capital expense is all up-front. A business model like this cannot be bootstrapped. USi raised a large syndicate of venture capital to start with and had several follow-up rounds of debt and equity before going public.

Not all ventures are VC plays. It is a good idea to assess whether your venture is a fit for traditional VC before trying to pursue it. Generally, a company will need to have the following, as a minimum:

- a ready-to-go product with proof of market acceptance;
- a large and growing market segment;
- a solid proprietary position or high barrier to competition;
- customers and revenue that speak well of the product;
- knowledge that the VC will drive the company toward an exit strategy;
- a market lead or potential market lead;
- lack of direct entrenched competition;
- an established team that is reasonably complete;
- experience in the industry;
- willingness to bring in a CEO from outside if founders don't have the experience;
- high integrity, good communication skills, cooperative attitude; and finally
- an understanding of the responsibility of taking outside money.

Most companies do not qualify. If you are one, then acknowledge it and immediately seek financing in other ways. For example, if you have an intellectual property holding company that brokers technology, it is unlikely to be financed by venture capital. Perhaps a private placement would be a better route. Or, if you have a government contracting firm, a computer reseller or a me-too venture, again, it is not a venture capital play due to lack of proprietary position. That does not mean it's not a worthy business. Go fund it in another way.

Understanding Venture Capitalists

Before discussing how to organize a venture capital campaign, there are a few things about venture capitalists that you should understand. VCs are investing other people's money, not their own. They are tasked with making a high return and are working for their investors, not for you. They will not touch your deal if they cannot manage you to some extent, if you are inflexible, if you are stubborn, arrogant, or otherwise scary to them.

Venture capitalists are in the service business, not just the business of providing cash. They like to help recruit staff, make contacts, and assist with budgeting.

Venture capitalists will not invest in you if you do not respect them and do not value their input on how to make money. They will not invest at your valuation; they will invest at theirs, which may be substantially lower than yours may be. If you are greedy for valuation, don't bother with VCs. If you want a partner to help you and you don't mind generously sharing with the VC fund, then it may be a good idea. You are trading upside for risk reduction and improved probability of success. Remember, 100 percent of zero is still zero. And 80 percent of all new ventures or more fail. Don't be greedy. Be reasonable. They will not invest if your market is too small, if your product is not proven, if customers don't like it, or if you don't have the right people on staff.

The VC world is a very small community—even in Silicon Valley. It is competitive but collegial. VCs will quickly size you up and then they will talk to each other. They wait for reassurance from other VCs before they invest. If you make a bad impression on one, then several others may hear about it and reject your request for a meeting. This is frustrating, but it's the reality. They will assess you to determine if you tell the truth without embellishment. They frown on pressure of any sort or entrepreneurs who try to play one VC against another. They will assess you to see if you listen, make eye contact, have social grace, and look like you'll get respect from Wall Street. If they perceive that you don't have what it takes, they will determine if you will accept an outside CEO. They will want your business plan and they will not sign a nondisclosure agreement as a matter of policy. You should not expect them to and your business plan should be prepared accordingly. You cannot rush their investment process, no matter how much you need the cash.

If you want to play, you have to play by their rules. It's not so bad if you are a team player. It may be a nightmare for you if you are a control freak, arrogant, or otherwise just want their money and don't want their help. Venture capitalists are in the service business, not just the business of providing cash. They like to help recruit staff, make contacts, assist with budgeting, and seek potential alliances for you. They will assess your team and watch your cash flow and product progress. Their goals are aligned with your, not against. If you are in the fortunate position of having a venture that is fundable by venture capital, you probably should go for it, assuming you have the right investor. Your chances of a successful exit are much greater with a venture capitalist than without one.

Executing the VC Campaign

The best time to look for venture capital is when you don't need it. Further, the best times are when the funds are plentiful. This may sound like counterintuitive advice, but if you wait until you need it, you will encounter several problems. It can take many months to close a round of venture funding, sometimes more than six months. Your company needs to be healthy during those months. Further, your desperation will make you look weak and put you in a weak negotiating position. Lastly, you may run out of money at a time when venture capital is not plentiful and funds are holding back to feed their existing portfolios instead of making new investments. So, the right time is when you don't need it. Otherwise, you may find yourself desperately seeking venture capital.

There are a number of time-consuming housekeeping items you must have prepared in order to execute a successful venture capital campaign. The following lists the highlights:

1. The business plan—your business plan should be completed including a polished executive summary and a five-year financial projection.
2. Business in order—Is your product or prototype complete? Do you have customers, references, and revenue, including some with strong names?
3. Target list—Have you researched the venture capital community and do you know whom you will contact? See the discussion below about doing your homework.
4. Valuation—Are you prepared for the kind of valuation you will have to live with from a VC? Are you even aware of the valuation ranges they will invest in your industry and stage? More homework.
5. Investment banker—Do you have or need an investment banker? Normally, this is not needed or desired at the start-up stage, but generally is a plus at the mezzanine stage (the last stage before IPO). If so, have you spent the time to prepare with them?
6. Presentation—Have you planned, prepared, and rehearsed a PowerPoint summary presentation that lasts longer than twenty to thirty minutes?

Before launching your campaign, it is essential to know with whom you are meeting. There are many firms and they all have different funds with different investment strategies. It is important to identify firms that invest in the same industry, stage of development, and geographic region as your own. First, do your homework and prepare a list. Second, call the firms directly and find out the status of their funds and current interests.

And lastly, call some of the companies in whom they have invested to learn about their style. You need to do your due diligence to get the right funds. Then try to find a credible source to introduce you to each firm. That may be your law firm, accounting firm, advisors, or others you know. Most cold calls in the venture capital world are ignored. Referrals get much more attention. It is well worth the time.

Valuation is an emotionally charged topic that calls off venture capital searches faster than any other factor. Entrepreneurs are often unrealistic and will send the VCs away immediately if they receive a valuation lower than their expectations. You may have fabulous technology, but a seed stage venture is not worth $10 million or even close to it. A lack of realism is the kiss of death when it comes to raising money. Seed stage and early stage companies are tough to value. Nobody believes in the discounted cash flow method any more because it can be forged into whatever you want. Using the financial performance of comparable companies is more realistic.

> **Valuation is an emotionally charged topic that calls off venture capital searches faster than any other factor. Entrepreneurs are often unrealistic and will send the VCs away immediately if they receive a valuation lower than their expectations.**

Whatever the numbers, you will almost always have to take less than you think. But keep this in mind. Valuation is important—but it's not everything. If you get offered somewhat less than you expect, you can probably make up the difference in less than a year's time during your hyper-growth years. You are negotiating over how many months you have to work before exiting, not over money as it appears. Do what it takes to get the money. This does not mean give your company away or go with the wrong investor. But weigh other factors more than valuation. How much help will you get with leads, introductions, strategy, recruiting, sales, and finance? Can they fund future rounds? What is their reputation and success rate? These things are much more important than a dollar amount.

A smartly planned venture capital campaign is conducted in a concentrated period of time. It begins with a two- or three-week period of having your executive summary referred to key partners at the firms that are being targeted. Based on the executive summary, the targeted firms will either ask for a full business plan or tell you they are not interested. Allow another two to three weeks for the venture firms to review the business plan. At the end of the business plan reviews, some of them will ask for a face-to-face meeting. This is the critical step. You want to try to do all the face-to-face meetings also within a two- to three-week period. This will allow no time for a venture capitalist that is underwhelmed with your deal to poison your campaign through venture gossip. Nobody wants to invest in a company other VCs have trashed. It only takes one ill-informed opinion to ruin your chances. The cost savings and efficient use of management's time are also good reasons to wage a concentrated campaign.

One decision you will want to make is whether or not to use an investment banker or an advisor to organize and manage your campaign for you. Generally, there is not much benefit to a full investment banking approach for early stage money. Often the VCs will look negatively upon an entrepreneur who didn't do it himself or is paying investment banker fees at such an early stage. If you have never done this before, use an advisor or angel investor, but not a full-service investment bank. Once you're at the mezzanine stage, having an investment banker is a big plus as it helps to prepare you for going public, but not before. VCs do not like paying broker fees. Their money is going to the broker and the broker usually gets in the way of the deal and interaction with management.

There are numerous books devoted entirely to venture capital that cover the subject thoroughly. If you are going for venture capital and have never done so before, consider reading Steve Harmon's *Zero Gravity* for a look at Silicon Valley during the recent Internet boom. It was published before the Internet bubble burst, which must be kept in mind as you read. Kathleen Allen's *Launching New Ventures* is informative as well if you are looking for textbook level detail. Or try the Venture Capital Resource Directory at http://www.vfinance.com for many resources on raising venture capital.

Finding Non-VC Funding

What do you do if your venture does not qualify for VC play? How do you find funding in hard economic times to match your business and industry? This section looks at some alternatives to venture capital financing.

Alternatives to VC

The most common alternative to traditional venture capital is the private placement. This is a source of cash, but generally it is not smart money. It is just cash and it usually comes with a set of investors who do not know your business well and who will not be involved in your business. If you are the type of entrepreneur who just wants to be left alone after you get the money then perhaps this is the vehicle for you if you can sell it. And it may work fine until you hit a roadblock and your shareholders get impatient. This may be the best source of equity capital for early stage companies that are not able to raise venture capital.

If you cannot raise venture capital and you want smart money and patient money, the angel investment may be the way to go.

Early stage ventures with proprietary technology may be able to land a corporate investor much like Motorola's investment in ConQuest. This is an avenue that has advantages and disadvantages. One advantage is that you may get a higher valuation and a customer with the package. One of the disadvantages is that you may be required to be exclusive with the corporate partner for a period of time or perhaps give them an option to buy your company. The latter can be both an advantage and a disadvantage.

A creative option that a few firms have been successful with is the Direct Public Offering (DPO). When using a DPO, you must file a registration statement with the SEC just like an IPO, except that it will be shorter and less costly, but still slow and expensive relative to other ways of financing. The DPO allows you to sell to unaccredited investors and you may freely advertise your offering. This of course, is not true for a private placement to accredited investors. You may raise up to $5 million. The difficulty with DPOs is that you must sell them directly, it takes many shareholders to get the money, and there is no public listing afterwards unless you use a bulletin board for penny stocks. A disadvantage, if successful, is that you must do SEC reporting just like any other public company and you are subject to shareholder liabilities. It tends to work best when you are selling stock to your customers and there are a lot of them.

If you have adequate cash flow, there are two other options available to you, both of which are debt financing. If you have a large number of receivables and you experience a delay in collecting, you may be able to find a finance company that will factor your receivables. This means buying them at a discount in trade for immediate cash. Other than selling receivables, you may seek a traditional or SBA loan from a bank. This will require a strong business plan and a record of profitability. It is not usually a good route for early stage financing.

Lastly, you may choose to seek a buyer for your company. Usually if you openly solicit this, it will reduce your price. Mergers and acquisitions are discussed in more detail in Chapter 10.

Initial Public Offering

The ultimate nirvana for many entrepreneurs is the IPO. Most ventures never reach this stage. Also discussed in Chapter 10, the IPO should not be viewed as an exit for the principals in the firm. An IPO is a financing event. It is done primarily to raise money and create liquidity for shareholders.

The principals, of course, must stick around and run the company and for the most part hold their stock rather than sell when the IPO is complete.

The IPO should not be viewed as an exit for the principals in the firm. An IPO is a financing event.

The right time to do an IPO is after several years of steady growth and several quarters of profitability. This is a point when you are sufficiently sure that the risk of getting punished by the public for a market downturn is much less. You are making money and you know how to continue to make money. You are using the IPO for growth, not an exit or as public venture capital.

The cost of an IPO is high. Not only does it take about a half-million dollars to prepare for the IPO, the time commitment is considerable. Public reporting becomes an obligation. Quiet periods limit what you can say to the public. Liabilities go up dramatically. Your venture is subject to the public sentiment about your market segment and the market as a whole. One bad quarter can kill you.

An IPO can also be the most exhilarating day in the life of an entrepreneur. It is the crowning achievement. It is an ego trip. It is a large amount of cash to complete your mission. It is a branding event. Your company will be forever different. But it is not for every company and it can only be done in a good market.

Powerize.com attempted an IPO during the dot-com fury, but our timing and motive was off. Details of the story are in the box below. Read it for lessons learned.

Powerize.com IPO Attempt

Powerize.com was an early stage Internet company and in 1999 the company attempted to file for an IPO. At the time, Powerize's revenues were only $300,000 per quarter, but many dot-coms were filing for IPOs when they had no revenue at all. The IPO was attempted at this time to obtain cheap money while it was available and to use stock as currency to make acquisitions.

To prepare for an IPO, a firm must write a document called an S-1, which is a detailed filing statement for the SEC. This is done with extensive participation of your investment bankers, accountants, and lawyers and can be quite costly. Legal fees may well exceed $100,000, publishing fees may exceed $50,000 and accounting/audit fees may exceed $100,000. In addition, there are filing fees and many incidental fees. An IPO filing may cost $400,000 in total. Keep in mind that less than half of all filed IPOs actually succeed. Many are pulled before the launch and some do not successfully sell.

In preparation for the IPO we raised about $8 million in private capital. We used these funds to establish a new business model offering premium content for free based on advertising, to set up some high profile distribution channels, and land some bellwether customers. We moved at an unimaginable pace and in a matter of six weeks and we landed about eight or nine key deals.

The underwriter for the IPO was boutique banker in Baltimore. We chose them because of an alliance with our prior financial advisors and because we were too small for the larger banks. This proved to be a mistake. They were not at all committed to the process and during our drafting sessions, the banker sent in his junior trainees rather than the partner who signed the deal with us. Support from them was minimal. It appeared as if they viewed us as a kind of wild card bet.

After submission on an S-1 filing, the SEC takes thirty days or more to review it. The usual response will be several dozen questions and objections, which then must be run through your lawyers and accountants and responded to. This takes several more weeks. After an approval is finally obtained, only then can the road tour begin for selling stock to institutions. Your investment banker organizes this.

We got a timely response from the SEC with minimal questions, and as we prepared to do the IPO road tour, our banker halted the process. They became squeamish because Hoovers, a comparable IPO went out at $14 and settled to $12 in the after market. The banker then began asking us to add features to our Web site. The features they were asking for were quite random and infuriated our product managers.

The window for dot-com IPOs began to close and our banker began talking about a private placement. We fired them for their unprofessional approach to our deal. They released us from the agreement and we sought another investment banker for seeking private capital

We pulled the filing on our IPO as did many hopeful dot-coms and the market entered a new phase. About sixty days later, the Internet bubble burst on Wall Street and the bear market set in. In the end, we were better off not having gone public. We pursued it for all the wrong reasons, namely an opportunistic capital market. The filing and undoing of the IPO and the market visibility we were paying for mounted a bill in excess of $1 million. It could have been used for many other purposes, except that the investors who put the money in were also expecting an IPO. An era of Internet investing was over, for the better good of the market as a whole.

For companies who did successfully go public in early 1999, it became very popular to do secondary public offerings and public debt offerings very quickly. Many Internet firms amassed hundreds of millions of dollars this way. Today, many of these firms are gone. Most of them are worth less than 5 percent of their peak trading value. Like IPOs, secondary offerings and debt offerings have their proper place in a traditional market. They should be used for raising capital when a company has achieved the strength and staying power based on its own business performance first! What a novel idea.

Sell, Sell, Sell…

The best kind of money is always earned through good old fashion sales—assuming you have a good margin and aren't a commodity. There is only one requirement that makes an organization a business, and that is a customer. Often entrepreneurs get so wrapped up in raising money that they don't realize the same effort could have produced that money through sales. Never stop selling and always make that the first money you seek. If your passion is still there, you can sell. Your enthusiasm sells more than anything. Can you still tell the compelling story of your horizon? Selling is a major topic in Chapter 9.

Chapter 9

Growing the Company

"All growth depends upon activity. There is no development physically or intellectually without effort, and effort means work."
—*Calvin Coolidge*

Everything we have discussed so far in this book has been about how to start and build a new venture. This chapter is about how to grow a company once you have established it. Once you have completed your product, landed on your beachhead, and secured financing for your company, the next and most critical phase in the evolution of your business is to grow it from an early stage venture to a viable operating company. From this point your challenge will be to prove your business model, gain market acceptance, and capture market share to enable growth and ultimately satisfy your investors and yourself.

This chapter is multi-faceted. It will discuss not only how to grow the new venture, but also how to face competition, management changes, and possible market erosion due to changes in the market or technology. The methods of achieving growth that we shall explore are:

- Sales Growth—increase your exposure, volume, and close rate
- Market Pull—create market demand and a steady flow of new business

- New Markets—find new markets for your initial products
- New Products—establish new products for your existing markets
- Acquisitions—acquire synergistic companies that accelerate your growth

Achieving Sales Growth

After making early adopter and technology enthusiast sales, sooner or later you must turn your attention to achieving steady sales growth. Early adopter sales are exciting because they are the first paying customers. But most likely those sales will not produce a lot of revenue. You will probably find the majority of these customers through your own network or through trade show contacts or other sources in no particular methodical manner. As your product matures, new sales growth strategies will need to be developed and the pricing model solidified.

There are two strategies for getting your early revenue figures up. The first of these is to land a handful of very large accounts. The second strategy is to increase volume by growing marketing and sales power.

There are two strategies for getting early revenue figures up. The first is to land a handful of very large accounts. While this will not produce a sustainable revenue stream, it does extend your early adopter selling to a higher level to produce meaningful revenue. When we reached our hundredth customer at ConQuest, we realized that over 80 percent of the revenue came form only six customers. Had we seen that in advance, we would have focused more attention on the big fish and much less on the customers that provided only small amounts of revenue.

The second strategy is to increase volume through strong sales and marketing initiatives. Here you target your market segments methodically, put marketing campaigns in place to reach those segments, and build and train additional sales personnel as necessary to meet the plan. This strategy can potentially provide a long-term sustainable revenue growth to the company. However, it may take a long time to achieve and it may require a lot of experiments until you find the right formula or until the market is ready to broadly embrace your product. Unless you have one of those products that has tremendous appeal and you are struggling to fulfill the demand, this can be a slow and not always successful process.

In the strategy for achieving larger accounts, the process begins by targeting accounts that have a need for what your venture has to offer. Who can achieve a strategic business boost from your product? That is your target. Then a bit of strategic selling is needed. These larger accounts will require a lot of relationship building and handholding to land. You may need to make several visits or hold many meetings and interfaces between them and others at multiple levels within your company. Senior management attention is a must. Once these accounts are landed, they will tie up a lot of your resources. This is one of the trade-offs of focusing on a few mega-customers vs. many small customers who are treated identically. Ideally, a balance between the two will be achieved.

Closing larger accounts requires strategic selling. This means truly understanding their critical business needs from their point of view and tailoring your message to show how your product meets their needs. It may require extensive, long-term relationship building. You may need to secure a consulting service contract on an ongoing basis in addition to selling your product. Customization may become important. Large, six- or seven-figure accounts take a lot of work. These accounts are not sold by throwing a product over the wall and sending an invoice!

To increase growth rate and decrease costs, which is always a worthy goal, try a methodical effort to decrease the sales cycle and increase the close rate. Easier said than done, you say? Perhaps not. Once you have landed a few bellwether accounts, a careful introspective analysis of the sales cycles may reveal an approach that will be successful with future deals, enabling you to achieve both of these goals. Find out what steps in your sales effort were time consuming and were not necessary. Try to understand the flow of information, decision making, and events inside of the organization of your targeted customer. Look for areas where the process can be shortened. To increase the close rate, again try a few basic common sense tactics. Look for ways to better qualify your leads. Find early warning signals to weed out accounts that will likely never close. Find ways to get in front of decision-makers earlier and more consistently. Build your reference account base. These suggestions may sound like common sense, and they are. But often, they are never incorporated into business processes and are never accomplished.

It is important to note that selling a big customer for a large amount of revenue can often take just as long as selling a small to medium customer for a modest amount of revenue. Not understanding the sales cycle can bankrupt a company very quickly.

When is it time to hire more sales people and expand to more territories? This can best be tackled after your sales process is mastered on the early customers. Too often, zealous entrepreneurs who want to conquer the world fast will spend their capital and expand before they have this information. This is almost always a costly mistake causing more businesses to fail than to succeed. Your early customers provide you with a test market from which you can gather data on what works and what does not.

Once you have the information to expand efficiently, then it becomes a matter of careful business planning. Expanding too fast uses capital very quickly and poses higher risks. What worked for the first few major customers may not work again. Moving at a pace that allows you to change and adjust your course has a higher probability of success than blind expansion at breakneck speed.

Developing a Business Pump

It's nice to land big accounts and get an early boost. But the real test of your staying power is to establish a business pump or a repetitive flow of regular business. Beyond "big accounts," these include many stable, repetitive business accounts.

Managing for growth and managing a regular business pump is a different job than managing the creation and start-up of an enterprise. Each phase requires different skills. Sometimes, this means bringing in new talent, particularly if the early team cannot make the transition or is unwilling. It takes a team devoted to the numbers rather than raw creativity. They must replicate what works, drop what doesn't, be willing to change until they get it right, and then drive the numbers higher and higher while maintaining financial responsibility. This might be a good time to bring in an experienced VP Sales to augment the VP Marketing already in place.

Increasing Market Demand

To establish a business pump, a venture first needs to establish serious, repetitive, unambiguous demand for its products and services. This is no easy feat. It is the mark of a mature venture that has customers beyond early adopters. The first goal then is to reach this stage of product and customer maturity.

First, establish credibility for the product or service you deliver. It must have established and perceived value, above competitors in at least one area. Second, establish a reputation for excellent customer service. Without this you cannot possibly grow in volume. Then you must get the word out and be heard above the din in your marketplace. Many companies attempt this too soon, even before the first two steps have been accomplished. That approach will most certainly fail you. When you have surpassed the first two milestones, then an aggressive and fiscally responsible marketing campaign to achieve brand awareness, create demand, generate leads, and support sales is highly called for.

Prior to this point in time, a venture's marketing program should be heavily based on guerrilla marketing tactics that rely on smart, effort-full techniques that deliver a lot of bang for limited buck. Previously discussed examples include visiting analysts, seeking press coverage, making public speeches, attending inexpensive trade shows, and heavy personal networking at industry events within your niche. Having an excellent Web site and modest PR budget may help as well.

Assuming that now the growth phase is underway and that your product is maturing and is widely recognized as credible and valuable, it may be time to step up your efforts to increase market demand. Here are a few suggestions that you may consider. Refer to Chapter 7 for further discussion of these topics.

- Work the analysts and the press.
- Develop online marketing campaigns.
- Attend high-profile trade shows.
- Use professional agencies for PR and advertising (within reason).
- Measure the effectiveness of your marketing campaign.

A solid, well-planned, fully executed strategic and tactical marketing campaign that is highly targeted is fundamental to demand creation. A couple of warnings:

- Watch the marketing budget and cautiously avoid the mistakes made by dot-com ventures of over-investing in marketing too soon.
- Avoid becoming a PR flash-in-the-pan company that is all glitz and no substance.

Managing Growth

Extraordinary growth requires different management skills than zero stage upstarts. Andrew Grove in *High Output Management* applies manufacturing principles to discuss management productivity. He contends that applying these principles transforms the act of management into a disciplined activity of monitoring processes that lead to a desired business result. Methodical management processes of this kind must be in place to withstand hypergrowth. There will be no time for an ad hoc, fire drill style of management. When problems do occur, your managerial processes must indicate a swift resolution so they do not interrupt business.

One problem that management must be attuned to during periods of hypergrowth is the impact of cash flow. You must maintain careful control of the growth rate and apply careful financial monitoring, using a precisely timed model, to know and understand the pending cash flow impact. Each period has cash assumptions, and these reflect operational events or actions or decisions. A cash flow forecast is therefore a management tool for resource deployment. You must be able to calculate the timing of various cash events that will impact cash flow. If the event does not happen, then resources must not be deployed that were earmarked for that event. The CFO may be at the focal point of this activity, but all of management must be involved in accurately assessing the impact of growth on cash flow.

Methodical management processes must be in place to withstand hypergrowth. There will be no time for an ad hoc, fire drill style of management.

Understanding cash flows impact requires you to have the right systems in place. An early stage venture needs little more than a rudimentary accounting system, a database for company records, and basic IT resources. The needs of a larger, rapid-growth venture are quite different. Sophisticated forecasting and financial modeling are needed, perhaps with real time adjusting capability. Inventory and supply chain control may be needed, depending on the type of business. Automation of nearly every high-volume corporate transaction function must be in place. This requires an investment in IT and the effort to build out the systems and test them in advance of the hypergrowth phase. Not all companies have the luxury or foresight to do this, which can lead to utter chaos during such periods of success.

On top of all these needs for automation, process-oriented management, and methodical monitoring comes the need to constantly expand your staff and train them. The hiring and training process cannot be rushed, which increases the need for capital again.

In addition to the process of building the staff, there is a significant psychological impact on early staff that needs to be addressed. Early employees who made many decisions are being forced to play narrower, often less visible roles in a larger organization. This is a natural consequence of growth and success, but narrowing feels like a demotion to many people. The value of their stock options alone may not be enough to make them feel better. The newer employees are more traditional job seekers and less entrepreneurial than the founding team. They will be entering the company without the risk and sacrifice of the early time. Often these new employees who have had no history with the company will not understand the equity distribution to others who may seem less qualified, yet have much more equity due to early involvement. These are human resources and managerial psychology matters that must be addressed. Failure to address them can cause much turmoil and distraction at a later time.

The best way to address this is to set expectations up front. An early team needs to be told that they were chosen because they excel at the tasks needed to start a company, but as the company becomes more operational, their roles may become narrowed or repositioned as new staff is brought in to handle operational matters. This is a natural evolution of a venture and a sign that you have succeeded. If this is not addressed early in the start-up phase, it needs to be addressed later through direct and open dialog and not silent shunting.

Achieving Sales Projections

Perhaps there is no one greater source of frustration to an early stage entrepreneur than developing and managing to sales projections. There is no solid data to make the forecasts, which makes managing to your numbers almost impossible. You cannot base large-volume projections on errant sales. Your early sales may not be indicative of what the market will bear. They were deals that you cut directly. Reliable market data must be taken from a statistically significant sample from typical customers, not early adopters.

Forecasting takes historical data and measurable market trends and projects what can be done. If statistically significant historical data is just not available, how then can you reliably forecast? What inevitably happens is that the forecast becomes a motivational tool for the entrepreneur rather than a prediction of the performance of a business pump.

The value and the expected accuracy of sales projections take on a new role in a rapidly growing company. Early stage companies are notorious for not accurately forecasting sales and not making the numbers forecast, sometimes by orders of magnitude. This is because they have no data on which to base accurate forecasting, they are optimistic by necessity, and they are primarily in the business of creating and selling a vision.

A rapidly growing company, on the other hand, does have a sales history. Its product has matured to the point where people are buying it. There is a history of numbers for proper forecasting. Further, the business will not survive if the numbers for growth are not accurately known. There is little tolerance for poor forecasting or missing the numbers. If the company is already public, there is even less tolerance for not having this down cold. If the company is still private, this is an excellent time to establish good habits.

Outflanking the Competition

There are many things you can do to grow sales, ranging from adding more sales staff to adding new products or even new companies to your mix. But the landscape is not so linear. Your competition would like to stop you dead in your tracks. They may create obstacles to prevent you from realizing your horizon or they may soundly beat you in the market by gaining greater market share. Part of growing your company is accomplished by thwarting your competition.

Always keep an eye on your competition, which you should know very well by now. A dedicated competitive intelligence process should now be routine. Track their public filings, monitor their Web sites, see them at trade shows, track their news releases, use their products, talk to their customers, call them up, and keep your ear to the ground. Analyze and synthesize all this information to get a clear and accurate picture. Then form scenarios assuming the worst case and figure out how to defeat it. Don't kid yourself. This is time to respect your competition and not overestimate your own strength. You may think you have a better product, but you need to ask yourself the following questions and answer honestly. Who owns the market? Who is well funded? Who has brand? Who has distribution? What are the alternatives?

The ideal positioning is a side-step position. Instead of competing head-to-head with them, take advantage of their market blazing.

The second step to outflanking your competition is to formulate a powerful and effective strategy for positioning against them. You need to have a strategy for winning. The ideal positioning is a side-step position. Instead of competing head-to-head with them, take advantage of their market blazing. To do this, you play into your strength and focus on a segment that needs it, while leveraging the legitimacy of the market established by your competitors. If this can be done, you have good competition. For example, Powerize.com was often compared to Northern Light, a search engine company with a library of premium content. Sometimes the two companies would face each other on an enterprise deal, but this was rare. Northern Light appealed more to librarians and researchers, whereas Powerize.com was positioned for business end users. This is an example of side-step positioning where the competition helped more than it hurt by legitimizing the market.

If side-step positioning cannot be accomplished, you may be forced into more direct competition. This is not healthy competition because when it comes to a prospect, there is often a zero sum game in which no player can gain except at another's expense. It is more expensive for you and it engenders a lower close rate. Sometimes it is unavoidable, though. When you must engage in head-to-head combat, some of the preparatory steps include:

- Create an effective sales presentation well-pitted against the competitor.
- Build solid reference accounts and a large enough share of the market to be credible.
- Have a strong sales organization to develop new business so you avoid chasing the competitor by sniping at their customer base.
- Have bellwether reference accounts that are on your side. Figure out who they are and put enormous effort into those.
- Know when to walk away from a deal and walk away early when you are not going to win.

Expanding to New Market Segments

The best way to continue to grow is to do more of what is already working. Maybe this means more sales to your existing customers or more sales to new customers in your existing markets. Or it may mean adding geographic territories to your target audience base. But when is it time to establish totally new markets? Isn't this a way to grow? The answer to this is yes, it can be, but approach new markets with the same careful consideration as when you first started thinking about your business. When you start a totally new market that is different than anything you have done before, you essentially have a new start-up inside your established company. If there is indeed a compelling reason to expand into new markets, you should take small steps to avoid injecting a major risk in your established business. The risks are lowest when you are repeating a model that has worked for you.

James Cook in *The Start-Up Entrepreneur* identifies reasons why a successful start-up should diversify once it has reached its initial achievements and stability:

- Your business may experience a market or cyclical downturn.
- Competition may retard your growth.
- All businesses take periodic nose-dives—offset by other business units.
- Diversification is insurance against these.

This leads to the question, should your business diversify and grow or merge with a larger, more diversified, and potentially financially stronger company? The answer may depend on several things: your desire, market positioning, rate of market change, and financial strength. It is important to make the right decision based on good business rationale and honest assessment, not emotion and stubbornness.

Many companies talk of "expanding to Europe" when the market in the U.S. has not been thoroughly penetrated. These ideas are usually driven from ego or a desire to travel rather than solid business thinking. Expanding to Europe is a logical step for growth when the market has been proven in the U.S. and when there is a solid market potential in Europe. But the return on investment or vulnerability to competition has to be at the right level to justify the enormous investment in capital, time, and people that will be required to expand in this way.

Adding New Products

When is adding new products to the company a good way to grow? This is never an easy question to answer because of the possibility that a new product may drain investment dollars, suck up management time, dilute the focus of the company, and add additional risk. At the same time, a new product can add revenue and help grow the company. Here are some of the key considerations.

- Does the new product support the mission of the company?
- Can the new product be introduced in a timely manner and within the financial and managerial resources of the company?
- Will the existing customer base buy the new product?
- Is this the most optimal way to deploy resources to achieve your growth objective?
- Will you achieve greater sales volume by investing in a new product versus applying the same level of investment promoting your existing product line?

Your answer should be yes to these questions if you are going to proceed with a new product. There is a tendency in high-tech companies to constantly innovate and develop new things. There is a greater tendency to feel the need to constantly produce new ideas. This is good when considered a sign of engineering talent. But from a business perspective, consider the following. Each new product may dilute focus from prior products. Not only do they have to be developed but they also have to marketed, sold, and supported. New products are best when they use the same customer support network, the same sales and distribution channel, and ideally meet the needs of the same customers as your previous products. A new product can be like a new venture inside your company with all the inherent risks of a new venture. Unless your company is thirty times larger than the resources required for a new venture, the financial impact and dilution of focus will be noticed and potentially detrimental.

A new product can be like a new venture inside your company with all the inherent risks of a new venture.

One caution for new ventures who want more products: Watch out for becoming an idea factory, one that is long on ideas and short on execution. There is a difference between being creative and revolutionary and coming up with a new idea every day. Powerize.com faced this problem in its business development function. Faced with a fast-paced, ever-changing market, our business development staff wanted to define new products for nearly every new deal. Despite the creative thinking involved, this degree of instability is not manageable in volume. New product decisions need to be deliberate, carefully selected as the best of a large number of options, and launched at the right time, both financially and within the right market trend.

A company needs to stick to a few simple principles and become good at them. Your product expansions should be driven from your core competencies and a solid product management plan. Several years into product development at ConQuest, a government funding opportunity came along to do information retrieval by voice rather than by keyboard. We received the funding, but quickly learned that we were not good at speech processing and better at text processing. This particular contract did not get past the feasibility stage. We stuck to what we were best at and that ultimately served us quite well.

Acquisitions

Entrepreneurs sometimes dream of selling their business as an exit opportunity. This type of merger is discussed in Chapter 10. But sometimes there may be opportunities to acquire other firms. Perhaps your firm is funded and theirs is not. Or perhaps there is a strategic fit between the two companies that is compelling. Or perhaps the company you are considering acquiring is failing and you believe their assets are a worthy addition to your venture. Lastly, maybe your business plan has a roll-up strategy to buy a number of companies in the same industry to make a large company.

In this section we look briefly at when, how, and why to do acquisitions of smaller firms when your venture is still private. Acquisitions can be a valid way to grow, or they can be an abominable distraction. This depends upon the specific circumstances. Often it is less risky and cheaper to grow a capability yourself than to buy it. Before considering an acquisition opportunity, the following prerequisites must be in place:

- Is there a "hand in glove" strategic fit between the firm to be acquired and your business needs and your horizon?
- Does the venture to be acquired have intellectual property, or a customer base, or people that you cannot otherwise obtain directly? Do these assets enhance your competitive position or market share?
- Can you withstand the disruption in management time at this point in time?
- Do you have or can you raise the needed capital? Do you need the capital for other more pressing needs?
- Can you achieve the same results yourself through internal financing? If so, can you do so more quickly and more smoothly?
- Is the staff of the firm being acquired going to stay or go? Do you need them to make the acquisition work?
- How will the customers of the firm being acquired feel about the acquisition? Will this be a triggering event for them to cancel?

To further illustrate the issues that arise during an acquisition, the table below shows some of the pros and cons of acquiring smaller firms:

PROS	CONS
• Gain of new products or services • Gain of customer base • Gain of talented people • Increase in market share • Increase in competitive offering • Increase in revenue • Prevents competitors from acquiring a valuable asset	• Time-consuming • High risk of failure • Dilution of effort or focus • Capital cost or equity dilution • Hidden liabilities or problems • Blurring of identity • Worrying your existing employees

Acquisitions can be a valid way to grow, or they can be an abominable distraction.

In 1998, Powerize.com acquired two content services from the IBM Internet division known as IBM infoMarket™ and Lotus Newsstand™. These services collectively had established relationships with over 100 business publishers and over 1,000 publications. This acquisition is discussed strategically in Chapter 10. Here we mention some of the reasons it was done.

Relationships with publishers were slow to be established and sometimes required large up-front payments. The IBM deal enabled Powerize to obtain about 30,000 business documents from thousands of sources instantly. The acquisition was also made because of disappointing product performance and revenues on the company's first product.

The deal closed in May 1998. It took until April 1999 to integrate the two companies, update the business plan, and launch a truly integrated product. The resulting company had two separate offices, one in Maryland and one in Virginia. Further, it took an additional year to get all the bugs fully out, update the product, and reach revenues in excess of $1 million per calendar quarter. Despite the business reasons for the deal, the management distraction and ensuing internal politics that developed over having two separate small offices in a small company made the real value of the deal questionable. In the end, the deal enabled Powerize.com's ultimate exit, so it was worthwhile, but not without substantial pain.

Let us look at a couple of other mergers of small ventures to illustrate the rather different reasons they are done. In some cases, acquisitions are used as part of the business plan to form a large company with staying power based on market presence. For example, one of Powerize.com's suppliers was an Internet service provider now known as Interliant. Interliant was built on venture capital and the consolidation of a large number of small Internet service providers. The Internet service provider business is especially suited to a roll up because each company does almost the same thing but with different user bases or in different geographic areas.

Another reason to merge is if the end result produces a stronger company with a better chance of survival. Two such companies that merged based on this principle were eNeighbors, Inc. and Local Square. Both were private Internet companies, each with only modest capital. They both addressed local merchant commerce on the Web with differing but complementary strategies. In this deal, no cash traded hands, but owners of each of the respective companies now own shares in Digital Dominion, the combined company. Digital Dominion has a stronger management team, more customers and technology, and a better chance to survive than either company individually.

There are many reasons to do acquisitions and many reasons not to do acquisitions. For most ventures, acquisitions are expensive and a distraction and not the way to go. But, as outlined above, there are many cases where it does make sense. What is most important is that the reasons are well understood and this is the best alternative for the acquiring company.

Chapter 10

Navigating the Exit

"He who hesitates is not only lost, but miles from the next exit."
—Unknown

The minds of entrepreneurs, venture capitalists, employee option holders, and investors are often driven by two words: exit strategy. These words, of course, are often synonymous with two other words: cashing out. Or are they? As you may find out, sometimes an exit strategy represents cashing out for everyone *but* the entrepreneur. Furthermore, the frequent bandying of the words exit strategy may put pressure on you. If you have properly positioned your venture, then your passion for the business and the proper execution of your business plan comes first. The cash out will be a natural consequence of this effort, rather than your first and foremost goal. Interestingly enough, those entrepreneurs who place cashing out as their primary objective are less likely to see the money than those who care more about the venture itself. This chapter discusses various exit strategies, preparation for this monumental event, recognizing your opportunity, navigating the exit, and life after the exit.

Understanding the Exit

You may ask, what exactly is an exit? An exit is an event that allows one or more classes of shareholders to become liquid and move on to other things without disrupting the growth of the business. These shareholders usually do not include the original founders, at least not right away. In most exits, the key employees are expected to stay for a while. Oftentimes, there will be financial incentives for them to stay and/or disincentives to keep them from leaving.

Normally, an exit designates either an IPO or a merger with a larger company. These traditional exits are the ones for which investors look. An IPO creates a public market for the stock and enables investors to eventually sell at their own pace. To company principals, however, an IPO is a funding event. It provides significant capital for growth and is generally structured so that the principals must stick around for the long haul. IPOs do provide a certain level of credibility and economic status to the company that can be quite comforting. However, the majority of IPOs eventually trade below their offering price, and only a few of the quality companies soar to sustainable high levels.

An entrepreneur needs to differentiate between his or her exit and the exit for the investors. They are *not* one and the same. In the section below, we will discuss some means by which an entrepreneur can continue on, regardless of the company status. Such continuation, of course, is not always possible. It depends upon the extent to which the company relies on the entrepreneur.

> **An entrepreneur needs to differentiate between his or her exit and the exit for the investors. They are not one and the same.**

When is an exit necessary? In the case of shareholders, an exit is needed when they wish to become liquid. This exit could arise out of opportunism when a deal comes along, or out of need to get a major shareholder out. An exit for principals is needed when they no longer want to run the business or be actively involved. Such desires could be due to a major life change, a loss of passion for the business or a new interest.

In IPOs and mergers alike, the principals and key shareholders are usually restricted from trading for a period of time by Rule 144 or by contractual lockup. These subjects are complicated ones, explained at a summary level in the box below. Investment bankers and acquirers may place these and other more complex restrictions on you, your key employees, and your largest shareholders for various reasons. The main reasons are usually to keep you around and to avoid flooding the market with sell orders that exceed demand.

Rule 144 Stock and Lockups

In a merger with a public company or in an IPO, you will sometimes be left with stock that is restricted by Rule 144. This situation is a very technical one, governed by detailed SEC regulations. If you do end up as the holder of Rule 144 stock, you should consult your attorney to make sure that you understand the rights and limitations of your stock. In this sidebar, a layman's description of Rule 144 is provided to give you a basic background.

Rule 144 is the SEC regulation that applies to stock that is not "registered" with the SEC. In order for stock to be registered, a specific registration statement must be filed with the SEC identifying that particular stock as publicly tradable. In an IPO, this process is completed through an S-1 registration filing. For a company that is already public, it can be done through other SEC forms, such as the S-3.

If indeed your stock is not registered, you can find a legend on the back of the certificate stating that the securities are not covered by a specific registration statement under the Securities Act of 1933. In this case, the sale of your stock is governed by Rule 144.

Rule 144 requires that you wait for a holding period of at least one year before you sell the securities in a public market. You can always sell these securities privately, but this practice is almost always subject to discount from the market and, of course, requires that you have a specific buyer. At the end of one year, if you are still in possession of the stock, you must file an exemption with the SEC before selling it. Your broker can usually help with this procedure (but not necessarily—many consumer-oriented brokers do not have experience with restricted stock). When you make this filing, the public will have knowledge of the event. In fact, if a lot of people are filing for Rule 144 exemptions at once, the market will react accordingly and the price of the stock may drop, sometimes drastically. Similar results often occur when a lockup period expires after an IPO and insiders once again have access to the public market.

A lockup and Rule 144, however, are not one and the same. A lockup is a contractual agreement not to sell for a period of time, usually six months. Investment bankers normally request this agreement. They will underwrite an IPO to give their buyers/clients preferential access to the market for the stock. Stock that is locked up is often governed by Rule 144 as well, but in this case the shareholders have already held the stock more than a year and the lockup is simply needed to keep them out of the market.

When it comes to making an exit, it is necessary to match your objectives with realistic options. In some cases, you can arrange the exit in your original business plan. However, not all companies are IPO candidates and, in fact, most are not. Negotiating a merger requires a significant strategic match between the companies involved and, therefore, involves a certain amount of luck and timing.

How do you obtain an exit? You cannot force one. But you may choose to be ready to act when your opportunity comes along. If your ultimate goal is an IPO, a substantial amount of preparation is required. This preparation starts by building the company to the point where it is capable of doing an IPO. It must have a great story, a solid product, and steadily growing revenue. The market must be right. An investment banker must be willing to take you. The investment banker you choose will give you a list of things that the business has to do, some of which may take several quarters of business planning and growth to achieve.

Powerize.com filed for an IPO in 1999. This decision was made at a time when, by all traditional standards, the company had no business seeking an IPO. The quarterly revenue was only $300,000 just prior to filing and reached about $1.4 million one year later. Usually a company has $3 million plus in revenue with several profitable quarters before filing and this standard is currently on the rise. At the time, Powerize.com was seeking to take a ride on a capital market gone bananas. Fortunately, we missed the window of opportunity. This error was partially due to the experience with our investment banker, as described in Chapter 8. Nonetheless, we could have gone public at $12 per share and received an aftermarket punch to $24, but perhaps today we'd only be at $0.50 per share.

Finding a merger is also difficult if you are forcing the issue. It is possible to sign a deal with an investment banker and have them shop your company, but this approach often fails and can certainly reduce the asking price. VCs do not typically like deals that have been shopped around. They like fresh deals and it shows that the entrepreneur did not do their homework. Both ConQuest and Powerize exited in mergers with public companies. In both cases, the following prerequisites were achieved:

- The company was not actively looking for a merger.
- It had a quality product respected by its customers.
- It had several differentiating points in the market.
- The company's revenue stream was growing and approaching profitability.
- Several potential suitors approached the company at various times.

- The company said no to the first offer that was made.
- Once accepted, the company consciously and aggressively pursued the winning offer.

It is possible to sign a deal with an investment banker and have them shop your company, but this approach often fails and certainly reduces the asking price.

Excalibur became interested in buying ConQuest because it strategically chose to focus on text retrieval and search engines. Excalibur had a strong market position, but a weak product. ConQuest had a modest market position, with a strong product and good employees, complementing Excalibur. Before accepting the deal with Excalibur, ConQuest turned down offers made by several other suitors. The company was not initially looking for a merger, but due to its recognized technical strength, hot market, and as-of-yet small market position, many players competing for market share in text retrieval were seeking a deal. Two offers for a deal came from competitors, who were also rivals to Excalibur. The highest value exit will come when there are multiple bidders for the company. Getting to this scenario takes more than luck; it takes strategy.

It is normal for consolidation to occur in a high-growth market. Other companies may seek you if you have a strong technology, solid customer base, or qualified employees. In our case, we had all three. Aside from Excalibur, ConQuest also received offers to be bought by two government contractors. These offers were ridiculously low in price compared to the real players in the industry. In retrospect, government contractors have a different business model and they were attempting to buy a technology advantage for cheap. They are acquirers best suited for small companies with very strong technology, but otherwise weak on revenue or staff.

In the case of Powerize, Hoovers, Inc. became interested in buying the company in order to add content, revenue, and technology to its expanding business. Hoovers is a leading business information portal on the Web with an established brand. Powerize offered additional content and technology that would potentially help Hoovers maintain their market lead.

One of the major obstacles for young ventures when looking for an exit is an unrealistic valuation expectation. Most entrepreneurs think they are worth several times their actual value. A lot of emotion gets mixed up into this matter and many good deals are lost over it. Market conditions and who-is-seeking-who have a lot to do with valuation, as do revenue, technological strength, staying power, and the availability of alternative paths. One reason for outlandishly high valuation expectations is that often there are highly visible players in the market with extraordinary and unsustainable valuations. Entrepreneurs will often compare themselves to these players, despite the fact that it is an unrealistic comparison to make.

In *The Gorilla Game*, Geoffrey Moore suggests a rational way of thinking about high-tech valuations that encapsulates a lot of the disparities we encounter. Let his thinking guide you. Moore also provides advice as to whether you should merge or remain independent. Gorillas, or the largest players that dominate a market space, should remain independent. Most others should not. They also should not use a gorilla as a comparable for valuation.

Seeking Alternatives to Traditional Exits

There are a number of reasons that you may want to consider an alternative to a traditional exit. Perhaps you have shareholders who want out and you don't, at least not just yet. Maybe you want to retire or leave and your company is not ready to exit in the traditional sense. Or perhaps a new product line has taken a different direction in the market and needs to be spun out. The timing of market or shareholder events may not necessarily coincide with your own life plans.

If you are ready to leave, but your company is not ready to be sold or go public, you should move on and find a replacement for yourself, rather than remain trapped where you no longer want to be. Then you may choose to sell a small portion of your shares to the new management or to existing employees. In your parting agreement, you may state that the new CEO or management must agree to seek an exit for your shares by a specified point in time, whether through employee purchase, company buyback, piggybacking on a traditional exit, or a leveraged buyout.

Another situation arises when shareholders want out and you don't. Ideally, an IPO could be used to address this situation. In this scenario, you can continue to run your company as a public entity and the shareholders who want out can have access to the public market. However, an IPO is not always possible, depending upon the financial health of your company and market sentiment. If certain shareholders want out when there is no liquid market and they are not strong enough to force a sale of the company, another alternative you may consider is seeking a private sale of their equity. This sale could be made to existing shareholders, new investors, or the company itself. In this case, the shareholders who want out will have to prepare to take whatever the market will bear for private stock sold prematurely.

If you need cash, but it's still too early to exit, you may want to consider selling a portion of your stock to employees, existing shareholders, or the company. Perhaps the company is willing to take on some debt to reduce the number of outstanding shares. In this situation, you may continue to run the company or be employed there while deferring the sale of the majority of your stock until a liquidity event comes along. The immediate cash from a sale of a small portion of your ownership may be enough to relieve the financial need of the company.

Let's consider yet another situation. Unlike the others, this situation involves a need that is not financially driven. Perhaps instead your feelings about your business have changed; you are no longer passionate about what you do. You have a new passion or you want to move in a different direction than the company is moving. This predicament can sometimes be handled through a spinout of the business unit you want to run, or through a graceful departure after you have selected a replacement for yourself. In this case, your exit is deferred to a time that is good for the company, yet you can still move on to something else. However, this solution may have several drawbacks. If you have sold stock to people who place their trust in you and then you choose to leave, they may feel betrayed. Even if you find a replacement, it may be someone unfamiliar to the shareholders who initially invested in your company because of *you*. This circumstance is one that you must delicately manage. It can leave you open to shareholder lawsuits.

The Afterlife

You have cashed out. You have left, been fired, or your company doesn't exist anymore. In some sense, you feel that you have died. What now? Perhaps you have visions of greeting St. Peter at the gates, but you don't know if this uncertain future will be heaven, hell, or limbo. Garage Technology Ventures calls it heaven on their Web site. Is it? Perhaps now, you finally have to decide what you want to be when you grow up.

> **Perhaps you have visions of greeting St. Peter at the gates, but you don't know if this uncertain future will be heaven, hell, or limbo.**

If you are like most entrepreneurs, it will be of particular concern to you that, despite the fact that you're gone, the business that you founded continues to pursue the horizon you established. Because you originally established this venture with changing the world as your first objective, money alone will not satisfy you. The best way to insure that the business is in good hands is by either planning your successor early in the game or by carefully choosing your merger partner. Of course, it won't be you in charge anymore and things will inevitably be different. But this changeover in management does not mean that the mission can no longer be achieved. You will need to take a dose of reality before leaving the business behind. New organizations and management personnel change. Some are not competent. Decisions will be made from a different purview. You can expect your mission, as you originally saw it, to be only partially achieved. As discussed below, you may need to prepare for the process of letting go.

Finding Your Personal Horizon

Perhaps you have spent years on your venture. It has suddenly ended. This termination can mark the beginning of a radical change in your life. Whether or not you are plush with cash, you are suddenly in a situation where, day to day, your life is completely different. It probably lacks definition. It can feel very unfamiliar and almost eerie at first.

For years, you have planned your business. But did you plan your life? Do you know where your personal horizon lies? Some entrepreneurs find that they must keep on going. For these people, the label serial entrepreneur may be appropriate. Some will found ventures over and over again. On the other hand, many will say they have had enough and don't want to endure the pain again. This pain, the pain of starting a venture, is very real. It takes its toll on your relationships, family, stress level, and potentially your bank account.

Other entrepreneurs may choose to retire and never work again. This group is most likely in the minority, given the typical entrepreneur's nature. A popular alternative to retirement among many successful entrepreneurs is to advise less experienced entrepreneurs. This practice can be a way of sharing your knowledge and experience, while keeping one hand in the game without busting your backside again. If you are primarily a technical person, you may find that you have the need to go on and invent something new. All of these choices are worthy of consideration. The decision about your afterlife is a very personal one that you alone must make. It involves not only what you aspire to do, but how you want to live your life. Perhaps it's time to pay back the family and give them more of your time.

If your company merged with another player in the industry, you may be asked to continue running the company. In this situation, life will be different. You will have a boss. In some cases, you may be given the option of working for the new company in a different position. Most founders are willing to do this for awhile, but very few last long. They are simply too used to working for nobody but themselves. Employees of the original founders, on the other hand, often become long-term employees of the acquiring company.

Regardless of the path you choose you will have to face post-exit psychology. You are no longer in control and you no longer have people looking to you everyday for advice and direction. You may even have a spouse at home who has decided to give you some direction. Perhaps it's time to take care of the kids for awhile. There is a process of letting go that needs to take place. It may take some time before you are totally adjusted to normal life again.

Managing the Cash Out

A popular illusion is that on the day of the IPO or merger, the principals walk into the sunset with a bag full of money. Nothing could be further from the truth. Yes, it is an important milestone, and yes, the odds of you becoming wealthy have just increased dramatically. But unless your company was sold for cash, monetizing your stock may be a long, complicated process.

As we discussed earlier, you will most likely end up being the holder of restricted stock. In addition to the usual restrictions of Rule 144, you may have extra restrictions. If you are doing an IPO, you will be subject to a lockup. Furthermore, if you choose to stay with the company and you are an officer, you will be required to report to the SEC every time you sell. This restriction will usually cause the price of your stock to tank unless it is done with great care and finesse. You may be restricted to trading during a trading window of about ten days after quarterly earnings have been announced. And you must be very careful about the statements you make to the public, as you are an insider and deemed to have inside information.

Selling out for cash is the only immediate cash exit. Not only is this method in the limited minority of exits, but it is usually the method leading to a lower-priced exit.

If you are doing a merger, you may be subject to contractual commitments. Perhaps you will have an employment period that you must work before selling stock. You might have a volume restriction on how much stock you can sell. Or, maybe you will have an "earn out" clause that states that the selling price is based upon future performance and you do not have your stock or cash yet. Some of your stock may be held in escrow for a year or two to cover potential lawsuits. Regardless of circumstances, getting to the cash always takes time and has some risk built in, except when you are selling out for cash. Selling out for cash is the only immediate cash exit. Not only is this method in the limited minority of exits, but it is usually the method leading to a lower-priced exit.

One thing is for sure—investment banking firms and financial advisors will drive you nuts. Once your exit has been announced, over a dozen brokers will call you if you are named as a principal in the documents or on your Web site. But the best way to find the right investment account advisor and firm is through a referral. Perhaps you know the person because he or she was one of your underwriters, or someone you respect has referred him or her to you. Be sure to consider only a professional referral from someone like an account executive who has experience in dealing with accounts like yours. It is especially important that this person understands and has experience with restricted securities and concentrated stock positions. You may need to use derivatives, such as stock collars or short sales, to access cash before you can sell stock.

This book is clearly not about financial advice. But there is one piece of advice I am going to leave behind. When you get your hands on a lot of newfound cash, do not rush to spend it or dramatically change your lifestyle. Take your time and plan out what you want to do with your life. Get yourself a good financial planner and build a financial plan that matches your life goals. Then stick to the plan.

Advising Other Entrepreneurs

Many entrepreneurs who have cashed out choose to advise other entrepreneurs in their afterlife. There are several reasons they make this decision:

- Advising others is a way to stay active and involved while remaining independent.
- It makes it possible to evaluate risks prior to investing in a venture.
- It can be a good way to manage risks in a venture in which you have already invested.
- By advising other entrepreneurs, it is possible to build up equity and further increase your wealth.
- It can lead you to your next gig if you have chosen to be a serial entrepreneur.
- It is a way of giving back what you know and staying networked.

Regardless of your motivations, being an advisor is not for everyone who is a cashed-out entrepreneur. As in starting your own venture, you must have a passion for it in order to do it well. And not every successful or lucky entrepreneur is a good leader for other entrepreneurs. Randy Komisar, in *The Monk & the Riddle*, describes his life as an outsourced CEO, a kind of "in-your-face" investor who will guide you, ask the right questions, and mentor you through the Silicon Valley process and evolution of your company. He performs this service as his life's work, his primary passion.

There are a number of considerations to reflect upon when evaluating potential clients. It is important to seek out intellectually satisfying relationships involving people with whom you have good chemistry. There are a lot of crackpots that do not really want advisors—they just want your money and your resume. These are the relationships to avoid. Not all companies are potential IPOs. Part of the role of the advisor is to help find paths for worthy companies that are not necessarily IPO candidates. Another matter of relevance is how you agree to be paid. Start-up companies cannot afford to pay you cash. Equity is usually the method of choice, and perhaps some cash compensation is deferred to a later date. However, if deferred compensation accumulates, you can expect the next round of investors to ask you to convert it to equity.

Advising can be both satisfying and frustrating. It is not the same as being an entrepreneur. You are not in control. However, it does not have the pressure of being an entrepreneur. You own your time. Advising can keep you sharp and involved, and help you to find good people with whom you can work.

Designing a Life

Now that you have cashed out, you have the opportunity to design a life rather than a company. If you are financially independent, your choices are vast and so many that they may make your head spin. Take your time, don't rush to change quickly, and a new horizon will dawn.

About the Author

Edwin R. Addison is Managing General Partner with Infinity Venture Group and Adjunct Professor with Johns Hopkins University. He is an active high-technology entrepreneur, angel investor, and advisor to new ventures. He founded two high-tech ventures, orchestrated three mergers, and now serves as advisor to start-up companies involving several technologies and market segments.

In 1997 Addison founded Powerize, Inc., one of the first technology companies in the enterprise information portal industry, which he merged with Hoovers in 2000 for $22 million. Powerize raised $13 million in capital and grew from inception to a $6 million revenue run rate in three years with a staff of sixty.

In 1990 Addison founded ConQuest Software, a search engine company based on artificial intelligence technology, and served as its CEO. In

1994 Addison was named Entrepreneur of the Year by the Information Industry Association; his company also earned the distinctive Product of the Year award from *Washington Technology*. The following year, *Washington Technology* ranked ConQuest as #51 on the National Fast 500 list. After raising $5 million capital and achieving a $5-million profitable run rate, ConQuest was sold to Excalibur Technologies Corporation in July 1995 for $33 million.

Prior to 1990 Addison was employed by management consulting firm Booz Allen & Hamilton for two years and by Westinghouse Electric Corporation in various technical, marketing, and management positions for ten years.

Addison graduated from Virginia Tech in 1978 with a B.S. in Electrical Engineering and from Johns Hopkins University in 1980 with an M.S. in Engineering. He also did an industrial fellowship at MIT in 1985 to study artificial intelligence, and more recently he completed a Ph.D. in Computer Science. Addison has taught graduate courses in entrepreneurship, computer science, bioinformatics and electrical engineering as adjunct professor at Johns Hopkins University on a part-time basis. He resides with his wife, Kathy, and four children, Shelby, Lindsay, Evan and Claire in their two homes in Maryland and North Carolina.

The following list includes references within this book and some additional suggested reading. It is far from a comprehensive listing of all the good entrepreneurship books, however. Instead, it is intended to complement the material in this book. Note that some of these books may be out of print, but I have included them anyway if they have been good references or valuable sources of insight.

Abrahms, Rhonda. *The Successful Business Plan: Secrets and Strategies*. Palo Alto: Running R Media, 2000.

Albrecht, Karl. *The Northbound Train*. City: Amacom, 1994

Allen, Kathleen, *Launching New Ventures: An Entrepreneurial Approach*, 3rd ed. Boston: Houghton Mifflin, 2003

Brooks, Juile, and Barry Stevens. *How to Write A Successful Business Plan*. New York: Amacom, 1987

Bygraves, William. The *Portable MBA in Entrepreneurship*. New York: John Wiley, 1987

Christensen, Claton. *The Innovator's Dilemma*. New York: Harper Business, 1997

Cook, James. The *Start Up Entrepreneur*. New York: Perennial Library, 1983

Davidow, William. *Marketing High Technology*. New York: Free Press, 1986

Drucker, Peter. *Post Capitalist Society*. New York: Harper Business, 1993

Foster, Richard. *Innovation*. New York: Summit, 1986

Gates, Bill. *Business @ The Speed of Thought*. New York: Warner Books, 1999

Gates, Bill. *The Road Ahead*. New York: Viking, 1995

Gilder, George. *Microcosm*. New York: Touchstone, 1989

Gladstone, David. *Venture Capital Handbook*. Reston; Prentice Hall, 1983

Grove, Andrew. *High Output Management*. New York: Random House, 1983

Hagel, John, and Marc Singer. *Net Worth*. Boston: Harvard Business School Press, 1999

Henderson, Carter. *Winners*. New York: Henry Holt, 1985

Karrass, Chester. *The Negotiating Game*. New York: Harper Business, 1992

Kawasaki, Guy. *Rules for Revolutionaries*. New York: Harper Business, 1999

Komisar, Randy. *The Monk and the Riddle*. Boston: Harvard Business School Press, 2000

Levinson, Jay Conrad. *The Way of the Guerilla*. Boston: Houghton Mifflin, 1997

Lewis, Michael. *The New New Thing*. New York; Norton, New York, 2000

Malburg, Christopher. *The All-In-One Business Planning Guide*. Boston: Bob Adams, 1994

Miller, Robert, and Stephen Heiman. *Strategic Selling.* New York: Warner Books, 1985

Moore, G. *Crossing the Chasm.* New York: Harper Business, 1991

Moore, G. *The Gorilla Game.* New York: Harper Business, 1999

O'Donnell, Michael. *The Business Plan: A State of the Art Guide.* Wayward, MA: Lord Publishing, 1988

Perkins, Anthony, and Michael Perkins. *The Internet Bubble.* New York: Harper Business, 1999

Peters, Tom. *Thriving on Chaos.* New York: Alfred A. Knopf, 1987

Porter, Michael. *Competitive Advantage.* New York: Free Press, 1985

Riggs, Henry. *Managing High Technology Companies.* Belmont CA: Wadsworth, 1983

Robbins-Roth, Cynthia. *From Alchemy to IPO.* Cambridge: Perseus, 2000

Schwartz, Evan. *Digital Darwinism.* New York: Broadway Books, 1999

Schwartz, Peter; Leyden, Peter; and Joel Hyatt. *The Long Boom.* Reading MA: Perseus Books, 1999

Senge, Peter. *The Fifth Discipline.* New York: Doubleday, 1990

Tomasko, Robert. *Rethinking the Corporation.* New York: Amacom, 1993

0-595-26751-3